MAKING
EDWARDIAN
COSTUMES
FOR WOMEN

Suzanne Rowland

THE CROWOOD PRESS

First published in 2016 by
The Crowood Press Ltd
Ramsbury, Marlborough
Wiltshire SN8 2HR

www.crowood.com

British Library Cataloguing-in-Publication Data
A catalogue record for this book is available from the British Library.

ISBN 978 1 78500 102 4

Photographs by Benjamin Rowland
Illustrations by Joe McRae

Dedication
To my mother Shirley Fenn

Frontispiece: Evening gown by Ida Pritchard. (Worthing Museum and Art Gallery)

Typeset by Sharon Dainton, The Design Co-operative Ltd.
Printed and bound in India by Replika Press Pvt Ltd

Contents

Introduction   7
1   Edwardian Fashion and Dressmaking   9
2   Tools and Techniques   15
3   Fabrics, Measurements and Sizes   25
4   Split Drawers and Chemise   33
5   Flounced Petticoat   41
6   Blouse with Tucks and Lace Insertions   49
7   Two-Part Walking Dress   57
8   Day Dress   69
9   Evening Gown   83
10   Lined Cape   97
11   Evening Bag, Hat and Parasol   105
12   Wearing Edwardian Fashion   119

Suppliers   125
Bibliography   126
Acknowledgements   127
Index   128

Introduction

The selection of garments and accessories featured in this book are indicative of the kinds of projects made by an Edwardian dressmaker; this could have been a professional seamstress working from her own premises (it was a woman's profession), a lady's maid or a skilled hand batch-producing blouses by the dozen in a small workshop. Tailored outerwear and corsets have not been included because these were specialist areas outside of the dressmaker's realm of experience. The garments and accessories featured are either from the collection at Royal Pavilion & Museums, Brighton & Hove, or Worthing Museum and Art Gallery, which gives readers the opportunity to make appointments with either museum to view the original pieces. Using museum collections poses some limitations for the researcher; it is widely acknowledged that historical clothing most often worn is likely to have been discarded; clothing saved for best is generally what survives and therefore makes up the bulk of museum collections. Fortunately both museums have diverse collections. Worthing Museum is a treasure trove of handmade and department store clothing. Due to the foresight of curators the collection contains unique pieces of everyday fashion; some in stages of disrepair, some perfectly preserved. The Royal Pavilion & Museums' fashion and dress collection also holds examples of clothing from department stores from mid-range to high end. It contains a number of sub-collections, including the clothing of wealthy women such as Katherine Farebrother, Lady Desborough and the Messel family, who were dressed by the top London couture houses and professional dressmakers. Due to a longstanding association with both museums (as a volunteer at Brighton and as a museum educator at Worthing) I have been fortunate in developing a familiarity with the collections and I have benefited from having generous access to the collections for research.

The criteria I used in selecting museum garments were as follows: firstly, all projects had to be suitable for reproduction; secondly, all fabrics and trimmings could be sourced without too much difficulty. A further objective was that projects should be adaptable and so projects have suggestions on how to adapt garments to make them suitable for both wealthy, leisured women, and for poorer women whose choices were limited due to a low income.

The Edwardian era, if characterized by the reign of Edward VII, stretches neatly from the beginning to the end of the first decade of the twentieth century (1901–1910). The sartorial influence of Edward and Alexandra, who married in 1863, extends beyond these boundaries, and therefore this book will cover a wider period stretching from the mid-1890s up to the mid-1910s. During the Edwardian period British society was rigidly divided by class, but by the end of the period things were changing due to new developments in the workplace and in industry.

Three dresses included in the book span the Edwardian era: a two-part walking dress with fitted bodice and trailing skirt from the turn of the century, a lightweight cotton day dress with pouched bodice and full sleeves from the middle of the era and a later style 'Empire' line evening gown with beaded tulle panels.

Not all garments in the collections are dated and others have approximate dates only. A close look at the tools and techniques used in garment construction can help with dating. Garments made before the First World War often used metal hooks and eyes as closures on collars and plackets. Wartime restrictions on the use of metal made it difficult for the companies producing hooks and eyes to keep up with demand and led to a limitation of stock and an increase in prices. An advertisement in the garment manufacturing trade journal *The Drapers' Record*, 14 August 1914, by the firm Newey Bros Ltd, shows that the firm were reluctantly increasing the price of hooks and eyes due to a 'great advance' in the price of metal.

Researching projects began in the museum's archives with the clothes and accessories and developed to include a range of additional sources. Worthing Museum has a wide selection of Edwardian dressmaking manuals and journal features in the archives, which include *Isobel's Dressmaking at Home*, *Weldon's Illustrated Dressmaker* and *Weldon's Home Dressmaker*. They also have a boxed set of dressmaking booklets dating from 1914 to the early 1930s produced as a correspondence course by the Woman's Institute of Domestic Arts & Sciences, which was based in Scranton, Pennsylvania. The course offered a range of valuable instructions for dressmakers, from how to stock and manage a workroom to how to become more proficient in the skilful use of a needle and thread when embroidering monograms on lingerie. *The Drapers' Record* archive held at The London College of Fashion has been a useful source of research; further sources have included women's journals, Government Reports, social surveys, dressmaking manuals, costume reference books and museum visits. I was particularly inspired by Janet Arnold's comprehensive observations of museum dress captured in detailed sketches in *Patterns of Fashion 2* (1982). Anne Buck's careful study of garments and accessories made when she was Keeper of the Gallery of English Costume at Platt Hall, *Victorian Costume* (1961), was a further source of inspiration, as was Lou Taylor's exploration of the development of dress through object-focused research in *The Study of Dress History* (2002).

Left: Two fashionable evening gowns in pastel shades sketched by fashion illustrator Ida Pritchard. (Worthing Museum and Art Gallery)

Chapter 1
Edwardian Fashion and Dressmaking

FASHION FOR ALL

The defining shape of the Edwardian period is the S-shaped silhouette, which refers to the shape of a woman in profile. The flat-fronted corset, seen in advertisements from 1900 to 1908, provided the first layer of shaping to the body, although it did not shape in the extreme way suggested by corset advertisements. The 'Erect Form' corset was featured in The Drapers' Record *in 1902 and showed an exaggerated version of the fashionable shape with a tiny waist, large bosom and protruding rear end. Much of the exaggerated shaping of the S-shaped silhouette was achieved by the outer layers of clothing, which included pouched front blouses and skirts that were flat at the front, smooth over the hips, with soft pleats or gathers at the centre back sitting on top of a similarly shaped petticoat. High fitted collars, trailing skirts and large hats, all decorated with flounces and embellishments, completed the look. Edwardian fashion was not always practical, or indeed comfortable. The straight fronted corset had the effect of flattening the stomach and encouraging the lower back to arch. The trailing skirts could also be a hindrance, as recalled by the Prime Minister's daughter-in-law, Lady Cynthia Asquith, in her memoir* Remember and Be Glad:

> ... the discomfort of a walk in the rain in a sodden skirt that wound its wetness round your legs and chapped your ankles...Walking about the London streets trailing clouds of dust was horrid. I once found I had carried into the house a banana skin which had got caught up in the unstitched hem of my dress.

The shape of a sleeve was one of the most changeable features in fashion, although one constant feature was a tight fit around the armhole. Writing in the *New London Journal* in 1906, journalist Mrs Humphry wrote of sleeves that were inserted too far back and sleeves that were tight on the fleshy part of the arm, and other sleeves 'that would insist on being a mass of wrinkles, no matter what you did to coax or coerce them.'

For the fashion-conscious woman the influence of 'the latest fashions from Paris' cannot be overstated. Even cheap penny weekly *Home Chat* had a section entitled 'Our Paris Letter', a fashion feature written by the glamorously

Detail of a hand-painted fashion plate showing a green and white striped day dress from Barrance and Ford, Brighton, Ltd. (Peter Hinkins)

named correspondent Yvonne D'Ivoire. In March 1895 she wrote of her admiration for imitation tortoiseshell hairpins in the shape of tiny wings. Fashion tips from Paris also feature heavily in the upmarket weekly journal *The Ladies' Field* and were reported upon by the well-known fashion correspondent Mrs Eric Pritchard. On 3 February 1906, Mrs Pritchard described a new fashion for linen collars: 'Parisians have them made of immense height, of beautiful linen, with a distinctive cachet in a little handwork ... [which] adds a dainty little suggestion of refinement'.

For a wealthier woman, dressing in a complete ensemble from embroidered silk stockings to her immaculately coiffured hair was a time-consuming process. A lady's maid was essential to help with dressing, to carry out clothing repairs, and to make alterations. If a maid possessed good dressmaking skills she might also make a lady's underwear. The maid would be kept busy throughout the day and evening because Edwardian etiquette required several changes of clothing to fit each new social occasion. Cynthia Asquith recorded the garments needed for a typical country house visit in the early 1900s:

> A Friday-to-Monday party meant taking your 'Sunday best', two tweed coats and skirts with appropriate shirts, three evening frocks, three garments suitable for tea, your 'best hat' ... a riding habit and billycock hat, rows of indoor and outdoor shoes, boots and gaiters, numberless accessories in the way of petticoats, shawls, scarves, ornamental combs and wreaths, and a large bag in which to carry your embroidery about the house.

Left: Corset advertisement in *The Drapers' Record* showing an exaggerated form of the S-shaped silhouette, 1902. (© EMap and the London College of Fashion Archive)

The fashionable clothing worn by Katherine Sophia Farebrother (1857–1928), the wife of a Salisbury solicitor, features in the collection at Royal Pavilion & Museums, Brighton & Hove. The Farebrother collection consists of over twenty dresses and accessories. When her husband died in 1913, Katherine's clothes were packed away and she went into mourning until her own death in 1928. The collection remained undiscovered for over sixty years and only came to light during a house move. The Royal Pavilion & Museums' records contain information obtained from Katherine's grandson which provides an insight into her lifestyle: 'Besides herself, her husband and three children, she organized a household of four servants, interviewing the cook each morning at 10 o'clock.' It is fascinating to observe a collection of clothes belonging to one woman and to form a sense of her personal taste and her financial means. Katherine Farebrother was said to be a talented artist and the collection shows that she occasionally wore artistic dress. The bulk of the collection, however, is comprised of more conventional clothing purchased from smart London department stores such as Dickins and Jones, and Harvey Nichols. She also used the services of local dressmakers although she was apparently a good, plain needlewoman herself.

For women who were not wealthy enough to shop in smart London department stores it appears that there were still opportunities to partake in fashion. Young working-class women employed in the Birmingham and Coventry metal trades were observed by a health and safety inspector for a government report in 1908. The report provides conclusive evidence of factory workers wearing fashionable clothing. The inspector observed:

> There are hundreds of girls engaged at fairly clean work in the Birmingham and Coventry metal trades operating the lighter milling machines and lathes. Very many of these girls are arrayed in flimsy, stylish attire, including blouses with loose sleeves and trimmings, and the hair expanded loosely with strands escaping, either by accident or design, from their fastenings.

The report not unsurprisingly sounds disapproving of women wearing fashionable clothing to work. This relates to the looseness of their clothes and the possibility of something getting trapped in the machinery, and could also relate to the 'flimsy' nature of the garments. The idea of young working-class women wearing delicate clothing would imply that they were dressing outside of the expectations for someone from their class of society. In order to understand the spending habits of working-class families between 1909 and 1913 Maud Pember Reeves and other members of the Fabian Women's Group recorded the daily lives and budgets of families in Lambeth, East London, in the publication *Round About a Pound a Week*. All families had a husband in regular employment and survived on a basic income of about a pound a week. Pember Reeves was mystified by the lack of money for non-essentials like clothing, and concluded that if new clothes were bought then the already sparse weekly food budget would be reduced. For the majority of families clothing was either handed down, homemade or bought from a second-hand market stall. The everyday clothes worn by most Lambeth women were a blouse and patched skirt with a sacking apron tied on top.

Young unmarried working women were a significant group of consumers of fashionable clothing. Known as the 'New Woman' or 'Gibson Girl', after the fictional character drawn by American illustrator Charles Dana Gibson, they required smart and respectable clothing to enter the world of office work. The Gibson Girl was often depicted in illustrations wearing a masculine influenced shirt and tie whilst riding a bicycle. Such was the appeal of this character that *The Ladies' Field* featured a Gibson Girl shirt pattern available by mail order in 1903. *The Ladies' Field* described the Dana Gibson shirt as the 'highest triumph' in shirt evolution and keenly praised American women for demonstrating how to wear it. While the New Woman was a cultural step towards emancipation, the women's suffrage movement was a political one. Suffragette members of the Women's Social and Political Union (WSPU) were given advice on what to wear and this included a lightweight blouse and plain wool skirt, nothing that detracted from their important message.

DEPARTMENT STORES OFFERING MADE-TO-MEASURE

One of the first department stores was William Whiteley's Emporium, which opened in Westbourne Grove, London in the latter half of the mid-nineteenth century. Other stores followed in London's West End, which rapidly became a fashionable destination for shopping. Stores such as Debenhams and Freebody employed seamstresses in workrooms on the premises to make and alter clothing. The seamstresses are captured in two black and white photographs, now in the National Archives at Kew, in which women are shown sitting shoulder to shoulder around long tables, sewing by hand with electric lighting overhead. For customers unable to travel to the large department stores a mail order service was offered for patterns and part-made clothing that could be fitted at home and finished to suit the customer. Catalogues and bound volumes produced by the stores featured sketches of fashions rather than photographs; these presented women with a glamourized ideal version of femininity. Worthing Museum holds the archive of fashion illustrator Ida Pritchard who sketched promotional material for the Peter Robinson department store in London's Oxford Street between 1906 and 1914. She was a skilled illustrator who sketched plates in colour or monotone; her figures were stylized but not wildly unnatural.

The upmarket department store

Photograph of fashion illustrator Ida Pritchard. (Worthing Museum and Art Gallery)

the premises. Another option was to buy an 'unmade' robe which was a partly constructed gown adapted and finished to fit an individual customer.

Outside London, regional department stores in larger towns and cities offered similar services. Leeson and Vokins department store opened in Brighton in 1882 and by the Edwardian period was well established as a destination for purchasing the latest fashions. Royal Pavilion & Museums has a selection of clothing and accessories from the store including the

Marshall offered a mail order service catalogue in 1909. The company boldly stated, 'We believe that this catalogue will be appreciated by ladies living at a distance from London who wish to wear fashionable garments concurrently with the leaders of fashion in the principal cities of the world'. Dressmaking patterns by mail order were also available to those living abroad. In 1907 an advert in *The Queen* by the London firm Kentish encouraged 'ladies living in the country or colonies' to order smart tailor-made gowns with the promise of an accurate fit. In Knightsbridge, Harrods department store sold both readymade and made-to-measure fashions. Worthing Museum has a commemorative book celebrating the firm's Diamond Jubilee in 1909, which contains a section devoted to each department in the store. The dressmaking service gave customers the opportunity of choosing fabric and a pattern to have a garment made on

Advertisement for Kentish, Ladies' Tailor, for plain tailor-made or dressmaking gowns, *The Queen*, Saturday 20 July, 1907. (Worthing Museum and Art Gallery)

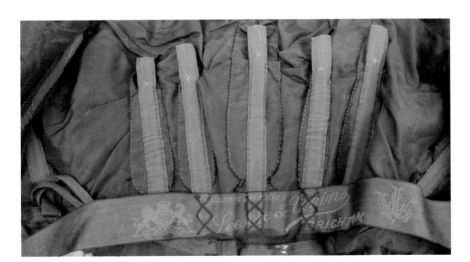

Internal view of the bodice of an evening gown showing fabric channels inserted with whalebones, finished at the ends with orange flossing. Waist stay woven with the name of the Brighton department store Leeson and Vokins. (Royal Pavilion & Museums, Brighton & Hove)

beaded evening bag recreated in Chapter 11. The University of Brighton's Design Archive holds the Vokins' Archive; this contains advertising materials and leaflets which demonstrate that customers were regularly invited to fashion shows to view the latest 'novelties' to arrive in store. Advertising materials stress that everything was sold at a reasonable price, which is useful for understanding the profile of the woman who might have purchased the beaded evening bag. Photographs of the store show well-stocked departments with rows of bentwood chairs for customers to rest in while an assistant attended to their needs.

DRESSMAKING

The ease of availability of paper patterns coupled with the rise in popularity of the domestic sewing machine allowed many women to make their own fashionable clothes at home. Weekly journal *The Ladies' Field* encouraged readers to try their hand at making their own clothes, in October 1907, by stressing the large variety of materials available and the advantage of getting a good fit.

Dressmaking was also a way for women to earn an income and the Edwardian dressmaker was a fixture in all levels of society, from Lucile (Lady Duff Gordon), designer and maker of beautiful and expensive gowns for society ladies, to an East End grocer's wife who earned a little extra money by making blouses for her neighbours. At the upper end of the market women could select a design from a hand-painted bound volume of designs. The beautiful autumn 1905 collection from Lucile is one example (reproduced in full in *Lucile Ltd: London, Paris, New York and Chicago, 1890s–1930s* by Valerie D. Mendes and Amy de la Haye). The Brighton-based dressmakers Barrance and Ford also produced bound volumes with a range of colourful fashion plates for customers to view at the shop or in their own homes. For women wanting to make their own clothes there was a range of

Front cover of *Weldon's Home Dressmaker*, No. 189, advertising free paper patterns of a Day Gown and Evening Dress. (Worthing Museum and Art Gallery)

dressmaking manuals offering tips and advice to improve skills or learn a new technique.

Edwardian paper patterns were often given away free with women's journals but this was not always the case. In 1901 the dressmaking journal *Isobel's Dressmaking At Home* advertised individual patterns for sale by post, claiming to be the cheapest in the world. An afternoon blouse pattern to buy was advertised at *6d* with free postage and packaging. One free pattern was included in this particular edition: a skirt with a bias-cut peplum. For younger women, wanting to make dressmaking their profession, an apprenticeship combined with an

education at a trade school was an option. In 1904 the Borough Polytechnic in south east London was offering a waistcoat-making course for girls as just one of several options. The social campaigner Clementina Black visited the school to learn about the benefits of educating girls in this way and wrote of seeing girls designing and making miniature sleeves and skirts that were then submitted to an advisory committee for comment and inspection. Making a miniature version was a method of testing a technique by using a minimal amount of fabric in a shorter space of time. Once the apprentices had qualified it was relatively easy to find work as a

Postcard of a young woman wearing a blouse and skirt with a straw hat, 1907. (Kat Williams)

dressmaker. There were disadvantages to the profession, however, because it was a seasonal trade, but the main disadvantage for women was the low rates of pay. A Government Report from the Select Committee on Home Work in 1908 provides information on the pay and working practices of makers such as 'Miss A' who had eighteen years' dressmaking experience. She worked on a 'fast sewing machine' which she had bought using the instalment system and paid for on a weekly basis. She worked long hours for a warehouse in the West End of London making blouses from home for which she earned between six and seven shillings a week, a very poor income at that time. Miss A explained the process of making a blouse to fit a specific size, which required a degree of skill. She received all pieces already cut out for each blouse and added the lace and all trimmings. It was important to make it to the correct size and she had a dress stand to ensure this was achieved. She explained, 'I have to put it on a stand, and shape the necks, and make it fit in all parts – make the arm-holes the right size, and make the necks to size.'

Domestic sewing machines were readily available to Edwardian dressmakers. On 26 September 1914 *The Drapers' Record* carried an advertisement for Jones Domestic Sewing Machines, described as silent, 'light-running' machines that could be operated by hand or by foot using a treadle table. More information about tools and techniques features in the following chapter. Chapter 3 focuses on a selection of fabrics and provides advice on taking measurements. Each subsequent chapter is dedicated to the recreation of a museum garment or accessory. The final chapter looks at the wearing of Edwardian fashion and gives ideas for combining the projects featured in the book to create a variety of new outfits.

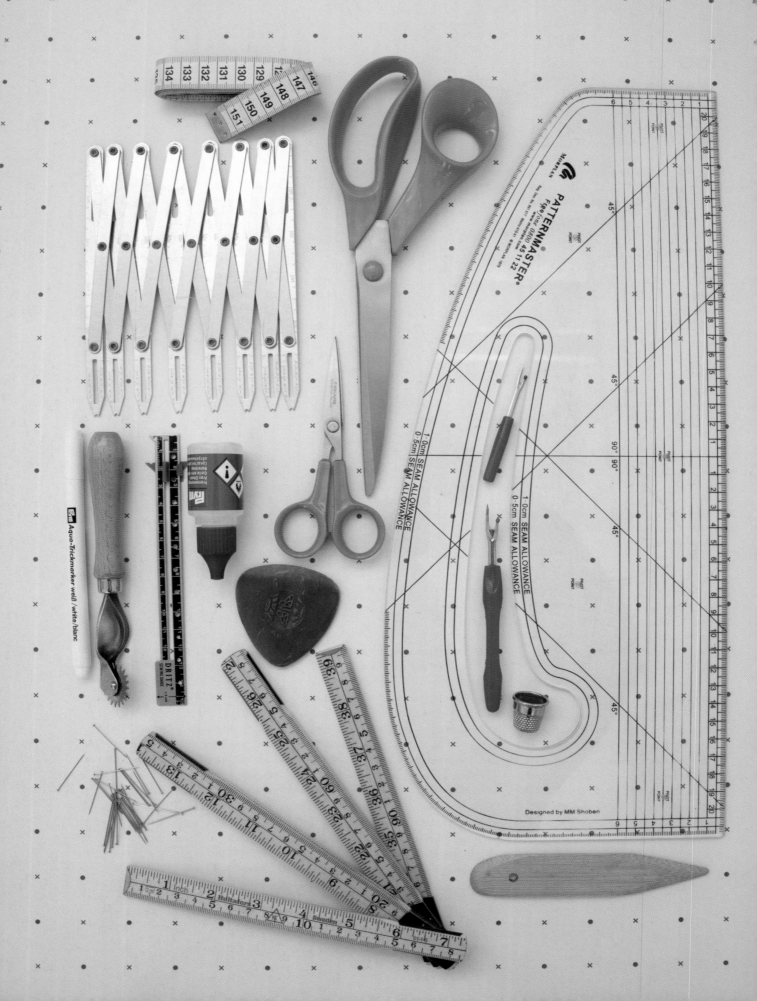

Chapter 2
Tools and Techniques

HOW TO USE THIS BOOK

The projects in this book are suited to those with sewing experience but I would encourage anyone with an interest to have a go at a project that they find interesting. The instructions for making have been written using my positive experiences of teaching dressmaking to many adult learners ranging from complete beginners to skilled makers. The techniques are all based on my experiences of working in theatre and film costume workrooms for many years. The advantage of working alongside skilled cutters and costume makers is that many tips are shared in a workroom, some of which I have been able to pass on in this book. All projects are presented with a series of step-by-step photographs and written instructions and, where possible, photographs showing details of the original museum garments and accessories have also been included. Breaking down projects into smaller tasks means that one section can be completed at a time and a good result achieved before moving to the next stage.

Once a project has been selected there is a list of materials, tools and equipment to help get started. Each chapter has a main photograph of the completed garment or accessory. Because some of the museum garments are in need of conservation it was not possible to mount them on mannequins to take photographs and so black-and-white illustrations showing detailed features of the original garments have been included. The sketches express the clothing as it is now, that is to say clothing that has been worn and used rather than in pristine condition. Specific instructions are given in each chapter on the cutting of fabrics and linings with a making sequence to

follow to achieve the best results. Additional information and hints on adapting garments for the stage, and for a range of social classes, is also provided at the end of each chapter. Many projects have some form of embellishment, including pin-tucks, tucks, ruffles and beading, which are enjoyable to create but also extremely time consuming. Where a technique is repeated, for example the beading pattern on both sides of the drawstring evening bag, only one side has been completed on the reproduction bag. Some garments have been slightly simplified, such as the blouse where there are fewer insertions of lace running down each sleeve. In each case this is explained, and descriptions and, where possible, photographs of sections of the original garments showing the techniques, are provided alongside the illustrations.

It is important to note that all patterns are reproduced without seam allowance and it is suggested that a generous seam allowance is added to patterns and trimmed down only after a fitting has taken place. If a true reconstruction of the inside of an original garment is desired then the finished seam allowance should be narrow. The seam allowance observed on most of the original garments was a scant 1cm, which allowed Edwardian dressmakers to be economical with their fabric. In theatre costume a much larger seam allowance is left to enable alterations at a later stage, for example if a production is revived with a new cast.

Taking patterns from original garments poses a few challenges: in some cases, due to the age of the garments, stretching, disintegration, wear and tear, and alterations may have

distorted the original garment. Even when a garment is in a good state of repair, allowances need to be made for the fact that Edwardian women differed in shape from women today due to a different combination of underwear, diet and exercise. The renowned theatrical costumier Jean Hunnisett studied paper patterns from French fashion journal *La Mode Illustrée* between 1900 and 1909 for her book *Period Costumes for Stage and Screen: Patterns for Women's Dress 1800–1909*, and noted that the Edwardian woman had a narrower back, a wider front and, perhaps not surprisingly, a smaller waist. Taking these concerns into account the patterns featured in the book are a contemporary adaptation of the Edwardian silhouette. The aim has been to retain the period look of each piece but to make the patterns suitable for a modern shape.

HOW TO USE THE PATTERNS

The scale used for all patterns is the same: one square = 5cm. The scale is printed next to each pattern. The following abbreviations and terms have been used on the pattern pieces:

CF – Centre Front
CB – Centre Back
SS – Side Seam
Grain Line – place the pattern piece on the fabric so that the grain line follows the straight grain of the fabric
Fold – place the pattern piece along a folded edge
Cut 2 – cut two pieces with the same pattern piece
Darts, tucks, gathering and balance points are also included on the patterns.

Left: Costume-making equipment.

How to enlarge patterns

The method suggested for scaling up the patterns in the book is to use pattern paper marked with a 1cm grid of squares. The best results will be achieved by working with only one pattern piece at a time and using a Pattern Master. Those proficient in scaling up using a photocopier will be aware that distortions can occur using this method. In all cases the pattern must be tested by making a toile and carrying out a fitting before cutting in fabric.

Adding seam allowances and transferring markings

Seam allowance is added directly to the fabric by tracing around the pattern pieces once they have been pinned to the fabric. How much seam allowance to add depends on the type of garment and what it is being made for. Commercial sewing patterns add 1.5cm to most seams but costume makers have to consider fittings and alterations and so at least 2cm should be left and more may be preferred. To add seam allowance to heavier fabrics and mounting fabrics, use a sharp piece of tailor's chalk to draw around the edge of the pattern. Also use tailor's chalk to mark darts and other balance marks. Once all pieces have seam allowance and have been cut out, marking can be transferred to the reverse side with carbon paper and a tracing wheel. For lighter fabrics, where the chalk and carbon paper will show through to the right side, temporary lines can be drawn with an air erasable marker. Thread tracing can be also be used, which involves tacking with double thread along a line, snipping the top threads, then carefully pulling the pieces apart and then snipping the threads between the two pieces. The making instructions in this book suggest pinning and then machining and do not include tacking in the process, although tacking can be included if required.

Making a toile and samples

Although it might seem like an additional and time-consuming process, making a toile actually saves time in the long run. A toile should be made before making up any projects in this book. A toile can be made from calico, muslin or similar fabric and all seams should be sewn with a long machine stitch to make unpicking easier afterwards. Toiles can be unpicked and the newly marked shape transferred to the pattern piece. As well as helping to test the fit of the pattern the toile can also be used to test techniques. Techniques can also be tested on smaller pieces of fabric to be used for a project. If pin-tucks or a flat felled seam have not been attempted before it is better to perfect the technique by making a sample before working on the actual garment and running the risk of having to unpick a mistake.

TOOLS

Having the right tools for a job makes the job easier; similarly, the wrong tools or poorly maintained tools add an extra level of difficulty. Many dressmaking tools and techniques used in the Edwardian era are still in use today. A further aspect to consider is a place in which to work. Ideally this would be a fully equipped workroom but many beautifully made garments have been created on a kitchen table. If you are lucky enough to have a workroom then a large cutting table at waist height is a useful aid.

Iron and board

A steam iron and a sturdy ironing board with a clean cover are essential items. A further useful item is a sleeve board, which can be used to press sleeve seams and small details. Theatre costume departments use industrial steam irons and ironing tables with a foot-operated vacuum press – this helps to hold the garment in place while the maker uses both hands for pressing. A pressing cloth made from a lightweight natural fabric can be used dry or damp as a barrier between the shiny surface of the iron and delicate or woollen fabrics. Fabrics require different temperatures and ironing techniques and it is worth testing a scrap of fabric before putting the iron on the actual garment.

All fabrics should be pressed before cutting. To achieve a professional looking garment each stage should be pressed in the making process before moving on to the next stage. Whilst work is in progress the garment should be folded over a hanger and kept neatly stored until completed.

Tailor's pressing tools

A tailor's ham is a cloth-covered pad that feels firm to the touch and (perhaps unsurprisingly) is shaped like a ham. It is useful for pressing hip seams or wherever there is a curved seam. A sleeve roll performs a similar function and is useful for inserting into sleeves to press seams. A tailor's pressing glove is useful for pressing garments on a dress stand. The padded glove or mitt is worn on the hand and placed inside the garment while the other hand operates the iron. For woollen fabrics a smooth block of wood known as a tailor's clapper can be used to 'block' or flatten an area directly after pressing. The block is held firmly in place for a few seconds after a burst of steam has been directed at the fabric.

Scissors

Scissors vary in size, with 8-, 10- or 12-inch blades; the longer blades are used by tailors and are also known as shears. Dressmaking scissors and shears are available for right- and left-handed users and should only be used for cutting cloth and threads. Three pairs of scissors are needed for the projects in this book: one for cutting out fabric, a separate pair for paper, and small, sharp scissors for cutting threads and buttonholes. For the Edwardian dressmaker the best scissors were those made from Sheffield Steel. An advertisement for the firm Cox & Co.

SEWING REQUISITES

Sheffield Steel Scissors

With Leather-Covered Handles for Cutting Out purposes, as Sketch, are supplied - -

In 6½ inch, at ...   .   **2/-** per pair.
 „ 7   „   „   ...   .   **2/6** „
 „ 7½   „   „   ...   .   **3/-** „

Buttonhole Chisels,
per doz. **6/-**

Large Bow Scissors,
six inch—per pair **1/6**

Buttonhole Scissors
per pair **1/-, 1/3, 1/6**

Needles. First quality, Sharps or Betweens   ...   .   per dozen packets **2/-**
  „   Prize Medal quality   ...   .   „   „   **1/6**
  „   Darners, Crewel, Wool, Rug, Embroidery, etc.   ...   ...   „   **1/- & 2/6**
Knitting Needles. Steel   ...   .   per gross **1/6**

Pins, Tapes, Thimbles, Samplers, Canvas, "Purity" Calicoes, and all Sewing Material, Cutting Out Papers, Needlework Blackboards, etc., etc.

SEE NEW CATALOGUE, JUST OUT.

COX & CO., SCHOOL CONTRACTORS, **99 & 101 NEW OXFORD ST., LONDON. W.C.**

Advertisement for a range of Sheffield Steel scissors in *The Lady's World.* (Worthing Museum and Art Gallery)

shows cutting scissors with leather covered handles and small buttonhole scissors, which would have been useful for cutting hand-worked buttonholes on delicate fabrics.

Seam ripper

No matter how experienced a maker is there is always the possibility of making a mistake when sewing. Edwardian dressmakers used a small sharp knife for ripping seams apart. A razor blade was another option. A tailor I used to work with used a small folding penknife for cutting threads, which hung from a piece of elastic tied to his belt. As an alternative a seam ripper (also known as an unpicker or stitch ripper) is available in two sizes. Small, sharp scissors can also be used.

Tape measure

A good quality tape measure printed in both metric and imperial measurements is an essential piece of equipment. A tape measure should not be wound into a tight swirl in case stretching should occur. Edwardian tape measures were advertised as being

60 inches long. A small sewing gauge is also useful for measuring small areas and for marking hems. The 'Picken dressmaker's gauge' was patented in 1915 and is described in the Woman's Institute of Domestic Arts & Sciences booklet *Essential Stitches and Seams*. It could be used for marking tucks, plaits and ruffles, as well as hems, buttons and buttonholes.

Expandable button spacer

This is a useful tool for working out the spacing of buttons, fastenings or pleats and was not something an Edwardian dressmaker had the benefit of owning. It is lightweight and folds away, and can easily be stored in the bottom of a workbox.

Long ruler

A metre-long ruler is valuable for measuring fabric and is essential for pattern cutting. A folding metre stick is lightweight and convenient for taking into archives (if allowed).

French curve

A flat curved tool used for drawing curved edges. The Pattern Master performs the same role and is another essential tool for costume makers.

Drafting paper

A roll of dot and cross paper marked at 1 inch or 2.5cm intervals is a worthwhile investment. Squared paper marked at 1cm intervals and plain newsprint can also be used.

Hand sewing needles

Hand sewing needles were an essential item of equipment for Edwardian dressmakers, some of whom did not have access to a sewing machine and therefore made whole garments by hand. The size of needle varied to suit each task with short, fine needles used for small stitches. Having the right sized needle was essential to complete each process skilfully and in good time. A good set of assorted needles is useful, with additional needles for specific jobs. For example beading needles are long and fine and fit through the opening of the tiniest bead.

Sewing threads

To replicate Edwardian garments accurately, natural sewing threads should be used. A 1902 advert for sewing thread in *The Drapers' Record* for Gütermann & Co. shows that the firm produced sewing silk and machine twist. Buttonhole twist was also available – this is a thicker thread used for hand sewing buttonholes. To match the colour of the sewing thread to the fabric, unroll the end of the thread and place it on top of the fabric (this should be done in natural light). If an exact match cannot be found then select a shade darker.

Fray Check

The Edwardian dressmaker certainly would not have heard of this product but it is invaluable to the contemporary costume maker. A dab of liquid Fray

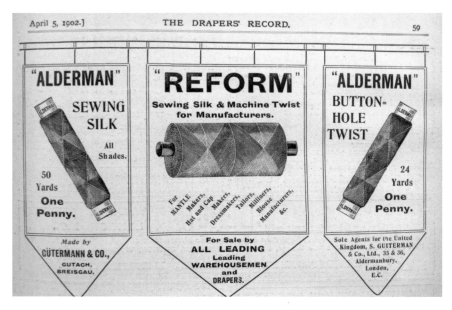

Advertisement in *The Drapers' Record* for 'REFORM' sewing silks and machine twist for manufacturers. (© EMap and the London College of Fashion Archive)

Check can be used to strengthen corners or to stop threads from fraying on delicate work. Other brands are available.

Bodkin

A bodkin is a flat, blunt needle with a large eye, useful for inserting ribbon through lace or elastic into a casing. A safety pin is an alternative suggestion.

Pins

'Cheap pins are not an economy,' warned the Woman's Institute of Domestic Arts & Sciences in *Essential Stitches and Seams*, and this is still the case. Cheap pins have a tendency to bend, break or rust and therefore stainless steel pins are the best option. Costume workrooms tend to use magnetic pincushions, which are also useful for picking pins up from the floor.

Turning tool

The social campaigner Clementina Black wrote in her study of women's working practices published in 1915, *Married Women's Work*, of collar makers in London performing the

'turning process' which was the act of turning the collar the right way round once it had been stitched. She observed that it was a tricky process and that most makers used a bone tool to poke the corners out to achieve a neat finish. A bamboo collar turner from Merchant & Mills is a useful modern equivalent.

Beeswax

Sewing thread is pulled through the edge of a block of beeswax to coat the thread with a layer of wax for extra strength. Tailors use beeswax for coating buttonhole twist when sewing a hand-worked buttonhole.

Thimble

A thimble protects the middle finger of either hand depending on whether the maker is right- or left-handed. Indentations in thimbles are there to make it easier to push the blunt end of the needle through fabric. Tailor's thimbles are open-ended because the tailor pushes the blunt end of the needle through layers of cloth and canvas with the side of the finger rather than the tip. The Woman's Institute of Domestic Arts & Sciences advised that

the thimble 'should not be tight enough to stop the circulation of blood in the finger, and yet not loose enough to drop off when you are sewing.' The Edwardian dressmaker had the option of purchasing a practical yet decorative thimble from a jeweller or 'fancy dealer'. The Dorcas thimble, for example, was made from three layers of steel and silver, not only to make it more comfortable but also to make it more resistant to damage.

Tailor's chalk and marking pens

Tailor's chalk is available in several colours, in either triangular or squared shapes. The edges of the tailor's chalk should always be kept sharp, either with a tailor's chalk sharpener or by using the blade of paper scissors. An alternative is an air erasable marker although it is advisable to test the marker on a scrap of the fabric before use. Water-soluble markers are also available.

Tracing wheel

There are two kinds of tracing wheel – blunt edged and sharp edged. Both are used to mark seam lines and construction points on fabric; the sharp edged wheel is useful for heavier fabrics. Carbon paper is placed underneath the fabric and all markings can be transferred to the reverse side of the fabric by wheeling along the lines. A self-healing cutting mat, a cork board or a heavy piece of cardboard placed behind will help protect work surfaces.

Light

Electric lighting was a feature used to entice machinists to apply for work in Edwardian factories. Advertisements in *The Drapers' Record* during the period often stressed this as an attractive feature for workers, alongside adequate ventilation. Sewing black fabric and close beading work still require a good workroom light.

Advertisement in *The Lady's World* for dress stands manufactured by John Clark & Co., London. (Worthing Museum and Art Gallery)

shaped red denim bag that was filled with emery, a tough material used for polishing metals. The emery bag was used to push a needle through when it became rough or made a squeaking sound.

Haberdashery box

For the wealthier Edwardian dressmakers, smart department stores such as Harrods offered a complete sewing kit in a custom-made walnut box which, like the decorative domestic sewing machine, would have complemented the furniture in the home. The kit contained sewing threads, buttons, needles, pins, mending cards, hooks and eyes, and thimbles. A modern and lightweight alternative is a small plastic toolbox.

Sewing machine

The lock-stitch sewing machine was widely available to the Edwardian dressmaker as either a hand or treadle version, or a powered machine. Machines had basic functions, for example the tension had to be adjusted for each new weight of material. In 1907 *The Ladies' Field* proclaimed that for the home dressmaker a Singer treadle machine was ideal. In 1908 the company released what was to become its most popular model: the Singer 66k. For those unable to afford the full price of a machine an instalment incentive was available. The weekly hire of a machine was another option. All projects in this book can be made on a domestic sewing machine or an industrial version. A domestic or industrial overlocker is also useful but not essential; the seams of Edwardian garments were either enclosed or overcast by hand.

Edwardian patterns

Edwardian tissue paper patterns had few, if any, pattern markings. Unmarked and unused brown tissue paper patterns remain with a few copies of the sewing journal *Weldon's Home Dressmaker* at Worthing

Dress stand

The Edwardian dressmaker was able to buy a variety of dress stands. An advertisement for Clark's dress stands in *The Lady's World* has a stand with padded, detachable and moveable arms, which sounds very useful. A cage in the shape of a skirt was another optional attachment for keeping the shape of the skirt without the need to add petticoats to the stand. A basic dress stand would be extremely useful for making the projects featured in this book. Stands can be increased in size by padding with wadding.

Emery bag

A piece of Edwardian sewing equipment no longer in use is the emery bag. The Woman's Institute of Domestic Arts & Sciences included the emery bag in their list of useful workroom tools. It was a strawberry-

Museum. The pattern pieces do not contain any balance marks or indication of the grain lines. In a 1901 edition of *Isobel's Dressmaking at Home* the straight grain is referred to as 'the straight way of the cloth'. The journal also states that directions for making up are stamped on each pattern piece and that if instructions are accurately followed 'success must be insured to the worker.' A small layout diagram to show the position of pattern pieces on fabric was also included. Patterns in this particular journal were only available in a medium size, which is described as 24-inch waist, 36-inch bust and 42-inch hips.

TECHNIQUES

Looking inside garments of the period reveals much about methods of construction. During my research, the discovery of entire garments with pin-tucks and lace insertions entirely made by hand was unexpected; likewise the discovery of many preformed fastenings and trimmings. It seems that dressmakers were either saving themselves time by using readymade goods or spending many hours on small-scale and time-consuming sewing jobs.

Taking patterns from existing garments and accessories

As a result of canvassing the opinion of a selection of experienced costumiers it became clear that experienced cutters and makers take patterns from garments in a variety of ways. With no universal agreement in use I decided to approach each project with the idea of using the method most suited to the garment and to the space I was working in, most usually a table in a museum archive. As the garments used are museum pieces I had to be as careful as possible when handling so as not to cause damage, wearing white cotton or latex gloves. For the accessories – hat, bag, parasol – I began by photographing the item from all angles. I then made sketches and

added measurements and notes on details. With the garments, I began by laying each piece flat on a table and photographing the garment with a front and back view. I then photographed details, which included embellishments, fastenings and linings. When possible I mounted each garment on a mannequin for further photographs. I found it useful to sketch each garment full size before sketching details and writing notes. This helped to draw the eye in to details not noticed at first glance. Through trial and error I found it useful to make a pro forma measurement sheet to allow for a methodical recording of details. One striking fact that emerged was that in most cases one visit was inadequate and it was necessary to visit the items a second and even third time.

The patterns were taken using a variety of techniques. One method was to place a garment on a flat surface lined with pattern paper and use fine pins and a pencil to carefully mark the outline of the garment. The exterior details such as frills and flaps were recorded by placing a piece of muslin on top. The muslin was larger than the detail and I pinned around the edge to mark the shape, checking alongside the measurements. I also followed the following advice, given by a range of experienced costumiers: for taking patterns establish the centre front and centre back of bodices and skirts. If possible, use light weights to keep the garment flat. For delicate garments hem weights would be ideal although this method is not advised for museum garments. When the basic pattern has been taken details can be checked (for example ensuring that all seams that meet are the same length). Use a straight edge and a Pattern Master to true up the pattern before cutting a toile. Put garments on mannequins if at all possible and even better use padded arms. It is also a really good idea to write a list of all measurements needed before visiting the museum, to avoid missing any vital information during the visit.

Tacking and basting

In *Cutting Out for Student Teachers*, author Amy K. Smith explained the process of tacking in 1910:

> Tacking stitches must never exceed three-eighths of an inch in length, under this is better. Stitches must be perfectly straight and should be worked very quickly. Commencement and finishing off are best done by back stitches, but if a knot be used it must be small and very neat.

A long thin darning needle was also recommended for tacking, threaded with fine cotton or machine silk in lengths not exceeding 24–28 inches. The problem of thread knotting can be avoided with the following piece of advice (passed on to me when I worked in the tailoring department of an opera house): 'knotting can be avoided by threading the end of the thread which comes from the reel, and not the one broken from the bulk of the cotton, which rubs the fibres of the thread the wrong way, and so encourages knots.' Basting cotton can be used for tacking and the advantage of basting cotton is that it breaks easily. It does not become embedded in the material and can be easily removed with tweezers if necessary. For a stage costume, it is not unknown for troublesome white tacking threads, impossible to remove in black wool fabric, to be coloured in with a black permanent marker.

Tailor's tacking and thread marking

It is essential to have a good solid knot rolled at the end of a length of thread to be used for tacking. To make a tailor's knot twist the thread around the forefinger of the left hand one-and-a-half times. Using the ends of the forefinger and thumb of the right hand roll the thread towards the end of the finger and slip off; the knot is then formed by sliding the knot off the finger using the nail of the middle finger of the right hand.

Tailor's tacks are used to transfer markings between two layers of fabric.

Using a double thread this temporary stitch is sewn through all layers of fabric and they look like a person swimming when first made – a round head and two longer arms. The loop is cut and then the fabric pulled gently apart and the inner threads are cut.

Thread marking involves making a long running stitch with a loose stitch on the top. This stitch is then snipped and the fabric is pulled gently apart and the inner threads are cut.

Grain lines

Grain lines were not always rigidly followed by Edwardian dressmakers, economy of material being the most likely reason. One example is the original skirt featured in Chapter 7: it has both back panels of the skirt cut on different grain lines; one is straight at the centre back and the joining panel is cut on the cross. To achieve the best results when making projects in this book it is necessary to follow the grain lines indicated on the patterns. To place a pattern piece on the straight grain of the fabric, fold the fabric in half lengthways making sure both selvedges are lined up. With the pattern piece sitting on top of the fabric place a pin at one end of the grain symbol and pivot the pattern piece until the line measures equal distances to the folded edge of the fabric. The fold is a more accurate straight edge than the selvedge; the selvedge can be uneven due to the manufacturing process.

Seams

Edwardian seams were very narrow. Unlike today, seams often used the selvedge because it was a more economical use of fabric. Open seams were used on the centre back seams of bodices; other bodice seams were narrow open seams pressed together to one side. Narrow flat felled seams and French seams were used on underwear and delicate clothing.

Rolling and whipping

Straight-sided lace was inserted between two pieces of fabric by first rolling a very narrow seam by hand and securing in place with a slipstitch. The lace was then sewn to the outside of the rolled edge by whipping or oversewing. This technique was used on the original Edwardian blouse in Chapter 6.

Hems

Skirt hems were approximately 10cm deep and formed by the addition of a separate, curved band or bias strip sewn to the edge of the hem and folded to the inside of the skirt. An additional braid was sewn to the inside of skirts worn outdoors known as a brush braid or plain wool braid.

Fittings

In a theatre wardrobe ideally two fittings would take place before a costume is finished. The first fitting is a garment in the early stages and the second fitting checks the fit before finishing. The fitting stage is a chance to eliminate any looseness and to check a garment sits in the correct place on the body. The length can also be corrected and any details such as the position of pockets and decorative trimmings can be checked.

Alterations and repairs

To make authentic-looking Edwardian garments evidence of an alteration or a repair could be added. For an Edwardian woman, a small tear or the appearance of an unsightly hole was no reason to discard a much-loved garment. The evening dress featured in Chapter 9 has a hole repaired in the foundation bodice with a patch and the centre back seam has been let out. It is likely that the bodice formed the basis of a previous gown and has been re-used.

DECORATIVE FINISHES

Faggoting

Faggoting was a tiny and narrow decorative stitch used to join two pieces of fabric together. Austrian cotton faggoting is a ready-made alternative.

Bobbles

Dangling, fabric-covered bobbles were a poplar decorative feature on both day and evening dresses. Both the day dress and evening dress featured in this book have decorative bobbles. Bobbles were made by gathering the edges of a circle of fabric over a soft lump of wool. Thread-covered bobbles, firm to the touch, feature along the edge of a belt that is part of a day dress from the collection of Marion May.

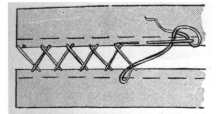

Fig. 64.—Simple Herringbone or Cat Stitch

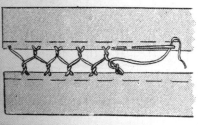

Fig. 65.—Fancy Faggoting.

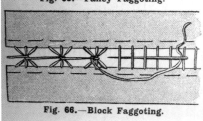

Fig. 66.—Block Faggoting.

Illustration of faggoting, a method of joining fabrics together, *Weldon's Ladies' Journal.* (Worthing Museum and Art Gallery)

Edge of a scarf decorated with a row of thread-covered bobbles. (Marion May)

Embroidery and beading

Beading was a popular decorative feature on Edwardian garments and accessories, especially on net, a lightweight fabric used to counterbalance the weight of the glass and jet beads. Embroidery also featured on garments, accessories and homewares. *Weldon's Practical Needlework* included embroidery patterns for readers to use at home; one fine example uses a mixture of satin stitch and couched ribbons to form a fuchsia design. Embroidery and beading requires specific tools and materials. Embroidery hoops come in a range of sizes and each suits a different job; for small motifs a small hoop is easier to handle. Small sharp scissors, small needles and a good light are also useful.

Couching

Couching is a way of securing threads to fabric using small stitches to overstich, useful for applying round braids and for sewing rows of beads in place.

Satin stitch

Satin stitch is a raised stitch sewn in parallel lines. It was often used for embroidering names and monograms on underwear, and for embroidering flowers and leaves and other trailing shapes seen on whitework.

Lace making

Women's journals provided lace-making instructions for readers to make their own lace at home for trimming underwear, children's clothes and edging household linens. *Weldon's Practical Needlework* featured instructions for making Torchon lace in crochet, which was to be executed in fine cotton with a steel crochet hook.

Tucks and pin-tucks

Tucks and pin-tucks were a decorative feature on many Edwardian garments and underwear. Tucks were also a means for allowing ease in a garment particularly if the tucks fell from the shoulder and stopped before the bust. As social campaigners Clementina Black and Mrs Carl Meyer observed, some factories had machines to sew neatly spaced rows of fine pin-tucks and this process would be done before the blouse pieces were given to the maker. For home dressmakers without this option, pin-tucks were formed by pinching the fabric to create a fold on the straight grain of the fabric and then sewing a running stitch formed of tiny stitches close to the edge.

Dying with tea

White fabrics discolour with age; a garment that looks ivory or cream now may once have been pristine white. If an aged look is the desired outcome white cotton lace or fabric can be dipped in tea (no milk) to achieve an ageing effect. It is advisable to experiment with a sample of tea solution before dipping the actual lace or fabric. It is not advisable to dip larger pieces of fabric because it is difficult to get an even coverage.

TIPS FOR DESIGNING AND MAKING COSTUMES FOR FILM AND THEATRE

This section contains interviews with two highly experienced practitioners, costume designer Frances Tempest and theatrical cutter and tailor Tony Rutherford.

Frances Tempest, costume designer

How authentic does a costume need to be for film? Is a period 'look' more important than factual accuracy?

It totally depends on the style of the film, and that's a collective decision created by the whole creative team! Sometimes complete period accuracy is what is required and sometimes an impression of the period is more important. Complete accuracy is out of fashion for costume design at the moment; relating to a contemporary style is the vogue.

As a designer, what draws you into a character?

Everything starts with the script. Then wide research, paintings, photos, advertisements, magazines, reading the social history of the period, etc. What one is trying to do is to embed the character into the narrative and tell the story of that character, so ultimately it should be a fusion of historical accuracy and telling details that will inform the audience about the character.

Finding authentic fabrics, lace and trimmings can be a problem. Would you suggest using vintage fabrics and trimmings if modern equivalents cannot be sourced?

Using vintage trimming usually helps to give a period look to a garment. Vintage fabrics and trims will behave in a way that modern ones just will not do as they are usually made from natural fabrics. Modern equivalents will sometimes work if they are distressed, boiled, dyed, broken down and generally have the 'newness' knocked out of them.

How important is underwear to the look of a costume? Would you specify a set of Edwardian underwear, including a corset for an Edwardian dress?

Silhouette is one of the most important ways in which a costume designer can place a garment into a period. The only way to achieve the correct graphic outline is to have the correct underpinnings. Original garments were made to be worn over a corset and will not work without one! There is also the psychological aspect of the actor feeling more 'in character' if the outfit is correct from the underwear up.

Do you have any other tips for people interested in designing and making costumes from the Edwardian period?

I am always struck by the fineness of detail in Edwardian garments and the scale of the trimmings, the fastenings, the embroidery etc. – all finely executed and daintier than anything produced post-1920. It was also the flowering of luxury, revealed in fine fabrics and impracticality: these women relied on others not just to launder and iron their clothes but also to physically dress them. Even the suffragettes, thought to have been practical and modern, appear to have worn what to modern eyes seem ridiculously elaborate blouses.

Tony Rutherford, theatrical cutter and tailor

How do you prepare wool before use?

I always steam wool before I start by hovering the iron just above the cloth. Sometimes you can see wool shrink before your eyes! It is an absolutely vital stage of the tailoring process.

Do you work in imperial or metric measurements?

I work in both depending on the cutting system that I am using. Older systems like those used in *The Tailor and Cutter* are in inches and more recent systems like Rundschau use centimetres.

What is your preferred method for scaling up a pattern from a costume reference book?

I prefer to use a grid to scale up patterns. I have tried scaling on the computer and printing the pages but a typical Janet Arnold page, for instance, prints out to nearly the size of my workroom wall! I always use the pattern as a guide to the shape and always make a toile to test the pattern before cutting into fabric.

Which reference books do you enjoy using?

It really depends on the period I am working on. The two Norah Waugh books are invaluable for any costume maker; *The Cut of Men's Clothes: 1600–1914*, and *The Cut of Women's Clothes: 1600–1930*. The V&A 'In Detail' books are really useful for close-up details of buttonholes, pockets, pleats and other details.

If you have to make costumes requiring a quick change what kinds of fastenings do you use?

Most usually a combination of snap fasteners and Velcro.

Theatre costumes have to be strong enough to last for repeat performances. How do you ensure costumes will last?

This really depends on the material but I would usually mount the top fabric onto a backing of cotton Silesia to make the finished garment more durable.

Chapter 3
Fabrics, Measurements and Sizes

INTRODUCTION

Fabrics

The fabrics included in this chapter are intended to give just a flavour of what was a vast range of fabric and trimmings choices for Edwardian dressmakers. Suggestions for suitable fabrics for the projects included in this book are made throughout, although in many cases it is not possible to replicate the original fabric, lace or trimming exactly, because they are no longer produced. Buying vintage fabrics and trimmings is an option but they can be time-consuming to source and expensive to buy. The white cotton I used for the underwear projects dates from the 1940s and was recently discovered in a shipping container, where it had been stored many years. It was marked in places but all stains were removed with washing and there are some imperfections in the weave, but this all adds to the authentic feel of the fabric. A list of the suppliers of fabrics, trimmings and equipment used for the projects is included at the end of the book. Fabric widths were not standardized in the Edwardian period and tended to be narrow, so quantities stated in dressmaking journals seem excessive even given that some Edwardian dresses, with full hems and frills, required a lot of material. One example is an evening gown featured in Isobel's Dressmaking at Home, *April 1901: 'Ten and a half yards of 22-inch satin...with eight yards of chiffon 44 inches wide'.*

Measurements

Metric units: metres (m), centimetres (cm) and millimetres (mm) are used throughout this book. The easiest way to convert to inches is to use a tape measure marked in both metric and imperial measurements. To convert measurements when drafting patterns, dot and cross pattern paper is recommended because this is marked at 2.5cm intervals, which is equivalent to 1 inch. Pattern paper divided into blocks of 5cm squares is also useful. The patterns included in this book are between a size 10 and 12 and have a 90–92cm bust and a 65–67cm waist. For alternative sizes all patterns can be graded up or down.

FABRICS AND TRIMMINGS

Dressmaking was prevalent in the Edwardian era and fabrics and trimmings were widely available, either from a department store, a local draper or a travelling salesman. The thrifty dressmaker could stock up on fabrics in the twice-yearly sales held in January and July. London department store Marshall and Snelgrove advertised in their 1910 catalogue a sale beginning on 3 January and lasting for three weeks.

Colours and prints

Edwardian fabric advertisements described a range of plain colours with poetic names – myrtle, bronze-green, heliotrope and ruby are just a few examples. Prints and woven fabrics were also popular; the day dress featured in Chapter 8 is made from striped cotton with a jacquard weave. In February 1906 *The Ladies' Field* reported on the craze for tartans in blouses and underskirts. In 1907 black and white checks of all sizes were popular for 'kilted skirts' worn with long black coats. Gingham and zephyr were manufactured from yarn that had been dyed before weaving and gingham in particular was marketed as a fabric that washed well. Subtle floral prints and sprig prints were also seen, although there is less evidence of their popularity in fashion editorials and advertisements. Royal Pavilion & Museums has a sprig print blouse in shades of blues and greens on a white background in the collection. A floral print dress also appeared in the bound volume of fashion plates produced by Barrance and Ford of Brighton Ltd, in shades of blue, green and pink.

In 1900 *The Lady's World* described a new pale blue cloth for sale in the Oxford Street department store D.H. Evans & Co. as resembling the blue paper used for telegrams at that time. *The Lady's World* said the colour was becoming to the complexion, unlike a recent fad for turquoise that was described as having an 'evil effect'. The idea of colours complementing the wearer's complexion was a common theme in advertising and editorials. White was a popular colour for Edwardian blouses; one reason for this was a perception that white was the most flattering colour to have next to the face. This idea appears to have been often enforced by fashion journalist Mrs Eric Pritchard. Writing in *The Ladies' Field* in November 1906, she claimed:

> White, and dead white in preference to cream still holds its own.... I have frequently referred to the fact that dead white is more becoming than cream. Where would the majority of

Left: A selection of fabrics and trimmings used for projects in the book.

25

Floral patterned gown from Barrance and Ford, Brighton, Ltd. (Peter Hinkins)

men be without the becoming clean white linen collar and cuffs? It is particularly becoming to the complexion.

As well as being 'becoming' to the complexion, white was also a highly fashionable colour. For example, in February 1908 *The Ladies' Field* reported that the wearing of white was increasing in popularity among smart and well-dressed women, which suggests that it was a symbol of status for the leisured classes. Black was also a fashionable colour as well as a signifier of mourning.

GLOSSARY OF FABRICS

This section includes fabrics used in the book and also a selection of the most popular fabrics mentioned in Edwardian fashion journals and advertising features.

COTTON
There were many different weights and qualities of cotton cloth produced in the Edwardian era, from the lightest weight cottons used for expensive underwear to coarser cottons used for cheaper garments.

CALICO
Plain, undyed and untreated cotton fabric, available in different weights inexpensive to buy and ideal for making toiles.

LONGCLOTH
A lightweight cotton also described as Indian longcloth, suggested in dressmaking journals as an alternative to silk for making delicate underwear.

MUSLIN
A loose weave, lightweight cotton fabric, used for mounting and lining in lightweight garments. Muslin can also be used to make toiles when a lighter fabric is required, for example muslin should be used to toile the blouse project featured in Chapter 6.

NAINSOOK
Nainsook is a fine cotton fabric often

Relatives of the author wearing mourning dress in c.1905. (Author's collection)

used for underwear. It was suggested in Edwardian dressmaking journals, alongside longcloth, as a cheaper alternative to silk when making lingerie or nightgowns.

PIQUE
Cotton or cotton-blend fabric woven with small raised geometric patterns, often used for sports clothing.

SILESIA
Silesia is a tightly woven, strong cotton fabric, which makes it ideal for pockets

and for mounting pattern pieces for costumes that need to be robust.

COUTIL
Corset fabric that can be used for a foundation bodice.

DOMETTE
A soft fabric used for interlinings.

FLANNEL
Flannel is an all-wool fabric, popularly used for Edwardian blouses and nightwear. It was often marketed as

being 'practically unshrinkable'. An advertisement in *The Drapers' Record* for Fred Doble & Sons of Dewsbury shows a mother and her daughter wearing long pastel-coloured nightgowns made from flannel in a homely setting.

FLANNELETTE
A brushed cotton fabric in a plain weave, it was soft to the touch and napped on one or both sides. Flannelette was a cheaper version of flannel and was often used for children's clothes.

LACE
Lace was an extremely popular fabric in the Edwardian era. The Edwardian dressmaker could buy instructions for making her own lace. *Weldon's Practical Needlework* had instructions for making Honiton lace, Torchon and guipure for trimming homemade underwear.

INSERTIONS
Insertions were strips of lace with two straight finished edges, used for trimming blouses and underwear. Insertion laces varied in thickness and width.

GUIPURE
Guipure lace is made when a pattern is embroidered on fabric and the fabric is then removed to leave a thick and heavy lace that stands up in relief. Guipure was either used as a whole piece or the motifs were cut away and applied as trimmings on blouses. Guipure is still available as either fabric or lace trimming.

CROCHET LACE
Crochet lace was worked with a small fine steel hook. Many sprigs, usually of leaves or flowers, were worked over a foundation cord. The spaces between the sprigs were joined by crochet bars. Irish crochet was particularly singled out for being of exceptional quality in fashion editorials.

VALENCIENNES
This is a flat bobbin lace worked with

Selection of lace used for projects in the book.

Postcard of the actress Kitty Gordon wearing a striped day dress with guipure lace motifs applied to the surface, 1904. (Author's collection)

one thread which forms both the design and the background.

TULLE AND NET

Net was used in Edwardian garments and accessories as a base for beading and for creating braids, which can be seen on the evening gown in Chapter 9 and the velvet toque in Chapter 11. Tulle is a finer form of net and was available in silk. Machine-made figured tulles such as *point d'esprit* were a popular choice for blouses towards the latter part of the Edwardian period. Writing in *The Lady's World* in 1900, 'Madame Modish' extolled the virtues of tulle for trimming a hat: 'Tulle is very perishable, but at the same time easily manoeuvred by the amateur'. She suggested combining colours to create a shading effect, for example pinks and mauves.

LINEN

Lightweight linen was used for blouses and summer dresses, while coarser weight linens were used as interlinings.

NUN'S VEILING

This is described in *Cutting Out for Student Teachers* as 'A thin, rather loosely woven plain material, with somewhat a rough dry appearance although soft to the touch. It washes admirably, and is durable considering its texture.' Collector Marion May has a nightgown with a square neck from the late Edwardian period with a label showing that it is made from nun's veiling. It feels soft to touch and would have kept the wearer warm through the night.

SATIN

The Ladies' Field advised readers in October 1907 that satin was the ideal fabric for a 'house-frock', which if worn with an embroidered scarf and under-bodice of lace or chiffon could even be suitable as a tea-gown to wear in the late afternoon.

SERGE

Serge was a hardwearing fabric used for outdoor clothing. An advert from Fred Doble & Sons of Dewsbury featured in *The Drapers' Record,* 31 May 1902, for their registered fabric 'storm serge' promised, 'sea water will not affect the colour'.

SILK

A variety of silk fabrics was available to the Edwardian dressmaker. Foulard was a soft twilled fabric used for dresses. Silk moirette was said to make a good petticoat. Lightweight silks were

Nightgown made from nun's veiling with a square neck embroidered with whitework. (Marion May)

Advertisement for 'Lewis's Wonderful Velveteen', a cheaper alternative to silk velvet, available to buy for two shillings a yard from Lewis's in Manchester. *Weldon's Home Dressmaker*, No. 112. (Worthing Museum and Art Gallery)

imported from China and Japan and used to make blouses. Widths of fabric varied between 21 inches and 36 inches. Chiffon was an opaque fabric originally made from silk but is now available made from artificial fibres.

VELVET

Both silk and cotton velvets were used for Edwardian garments and accessories. Velveteen was also advertised. In 1909 *The Lady's World* cautioned against using a heavy-weight velvet for hat making and suggested 'millinery weight' must be purchased. Unfortunately it is no longer possible to buy millinery weight velvet. Velveteen was a less expensive alternative to silk velvet.

VIYELLA

A trade name for a lightweight plain weave fabric composed of 45% cotton and 55% wool. Viyella was marketed as being pre-shrunk and therefore washable.

WOOL

Many varieties of wool were on sale to the Edwardian dressmaker; one lightweight example is Delaine, which was popular for winter blouses. Tweeds were popular for winter-weight tailor-made costumes and cloaks. The subtle colours of tweed fabric were much admired by *The Lady's World* in 1909; they could find not a single unpleasant shade.

INTERFACINGS AND BONING

From handling many Edwardian garments in museum collections it seems Edwardian dressmakers used little in the way of interfacing in lightweight clothing. Plackets, cuffs and facings are soft to the touch rather than firm, which would be expected if interfacing had been used. In jackets and costume bodices a layer of canvas was used to structure collars, cuffs and facings. Boning was often used, however, and can be found in collars, at the centre back of waistbands and attached in casings along the seams of bodices. Boning was of course used for shaping corsets, although some corsets designed specifically for playing sport were unboned.

PETERSHAM

When a straight waistband was applied to the waist of a skirt the method of adding structure was to insert Petersham ribbon. The original skirt featured in Chapter 7 has a waistband stiffened with Petersham ribbon.

Advertisement in *The Drapers' Record* for 'elegant' skirt facings with silk plush cord and real mohair brush edge. (© EMap and the London College of Fashion Archive)

Advertisement for Cash's Cambric Frillings, *The Queen*, 1907. (Worthing Museum and Art Gallery)

BRUSH BRAID

Brush braid was designed to protect the hem of an outdoor skirt and was hand sewn just inside the hem of the skirt all the way around the hem. An advertisement in *The Drapers' Record* in April 1902 shows braid made from either mohair or silk that was 'splendid wearing'.

Trimmings

In her book *Shops and Shopping, 1800–1914: Where, and in What Manner the Well-Dressed Englishwoman Bought Her Clothes*, Alison Adburgham explained that the haberdashery counter in a store was always located on the ground floor near to the entrance. It was understood that a customer might spend a small amount of money on trimmings and might then venture into the rest of the store and make larger purchases. The smart London department store Harrods had a Lace and Ribbon Department that was situated on the ground floor. According to a book commemorating the firm's diamond jubilee in 1909, customers could find

> ... rich examples of laces from all parts of Europe...Ribbons, Fancy Neckwear, Feather Stoles [and] departments devoted to haberdashery, trimming, Fancy Needlework, Artificial flowers, Parisian jewellery, Ladies' Hosiery, Gloves and shawls, the whole forming a galaxy of beautiful colour and fabric of extreme charm.

Edwardian clothing is known for its elaborate trimmings, frills and flounces, which gives the impression that dressmakers spent hours frilling lace, adding embroidery and layers of decoration. Some may have taken this route but there was an alternative – readymade frilled insertions. Cash's Coventry Frilling was advocated by dressmaking teacher and author Amy K. Smith in 1910:

> It has a gathered thread at the edge which enables the material to be drawn up, so as to make a regular distribution of fullness. The frilling can be bought ruffled into a straight

featherstitched band, which is a great saving of time, as the frilling is just ready to be sewn or machined to any garment.

It was reasonably priced, versatile and good quality and, crucially for undergarments, it could be washed and ironed. An advertisement for Cash's 'cambric frillings with drawing cord' features in *The Queen* in 1907 and readers were advised that it was of the finest quality, was durable and would last a long time. In 1908 *The Ladies' Field* extolled the virtues of Cash's colour-fast 'washing ribbons' available in two widths in shades of red, pink, blue, heliotrope and white.

Buttons and other fastenings

Decorative buttons were seen on women's clothing but were not used as often as hooks and bars or hooks and eyes as garment closures. The original walking dress featured in Chapter 7 has small flower-shaped jet buttons.

TAKING MEASUREMENTS

Edwardian women wore layers of underwear, including a fitted corset. Measurements taken for most of the projects in this book should be taken over appropriate foundation garments, but the drawers and chemise measurements are to be taken directly from the body. Use the following advice for taking measurements, record all measurements and include the name of the wearer.

Height – stand against a wall and with a ruler on top of your head make a small pencil mark on the wall. Measure from here down to the floor.

Collar – measure around the base of the neck (not tightly).

Bust – measure around the fullest part of the bust. The tape measure must be straight across the back.

Waist – tie tape around natural waistline (bend to the side to find this). Measure the waist firmly over the tape.

Hips – measure 7–9 inches or 18–23cm down from the waist tape at the side of your body to find the fullest part of your hips. Firmly measure around hips, keeping the tape the same distance from the waist all the way around.

Nape of neck to waist – tip the head forward to find the most prominent bone at the top of the spine and measure from here down the spine to the back waist.

Across back – measure across the back, passing the tape measure horizontally over the peak of the shoulder blades.

Shoulder – measure from the bone at the end of the shoulder to the base of the neck.

Sleeve – there are two methods for doing this: either measure from

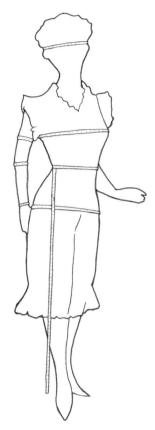

Front view illustration showing where to position the tape measure when measuring the head, bust, waist, hip, waist to floor, bicep, elbow and wrist.

Back view illustration showing where to position the tape measure when measuring the collar, across back and nape of neck to waist.

under the arm to the wrist then take off 3cm, or slightly bend the arm and measure from the tip of the shoulder to the wrist bone.

Bicep, elbow and wrist – measure quite loosely.

Waist to floor – measure from the side front waist to the floor. The finished hem measurement can also be taken in this way.

Head – measure around the circumference of the head.

Sizes

By observing museum garments, clothing advertisements and dressmaking patterns it can be noted that Edwardian women came in a variety of shapes and sizes. For example, a skirt advertisement from 1909 lists available hip sizes as being 36–42 inches. An online clip from 1917, briefly showing a fashion parade that included a gown by the British couturier Lucile, shows tall models, known as mannequins, of an above average size. The Brighton department store Leeson and Vokins offered a made-to-measure service for customers of all sizes; their garments were advertised as being 'made in several sizes...to fit any figure, including extra-large sizes'. In 1895 *Home Chat* listed their paper patterns as being available to order in three sizes; the largest was bust 40 inches and waist 28 inches, and the smallest was bust 34 inches and waist 22 inches. The length of skirt was a standard 41 inches for all sizes.

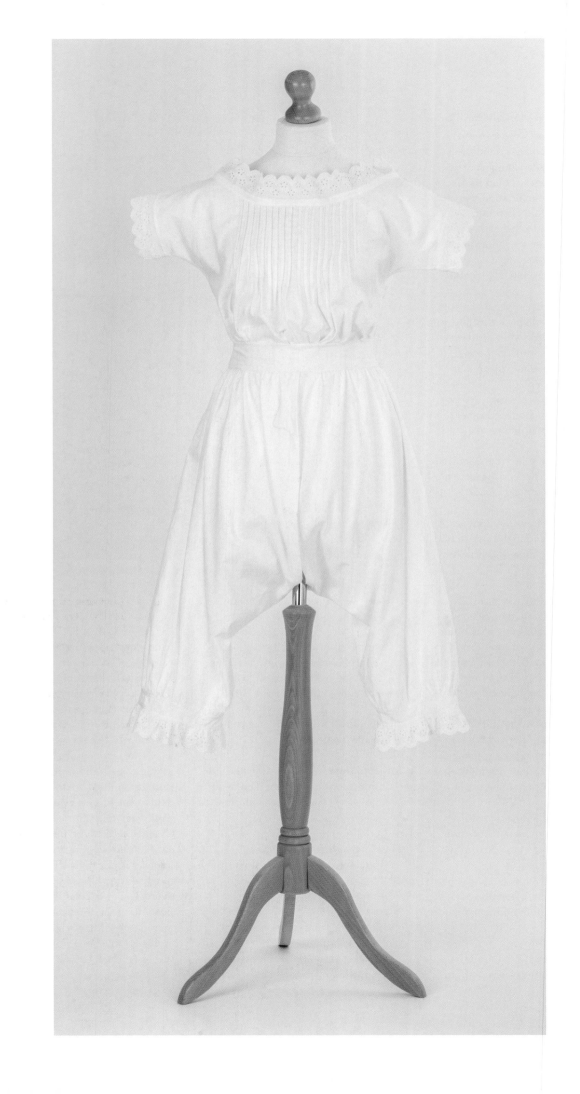

Chapter 4
Split Drawers and Chemise

Due to Edwardian conventions of etiquette and modesty it is difficult to ascertain just how many women preferred closed drawers and how many still wore split drawers. Advertising features had a tendency to show the drawers folded into a neat square with just the frilled edge around the bottom of the legs on display. Fashion articles in women's journals also tended to side-step the issue and therefore the dilemma for this chapter was whether to include closed or split drawers. Weldon's Ladies' Journal, July 1905, features a pattern for a pair of 'closed knickers', which it acknowledges are preferable to many women, with suggested fabrics being linen, alpaca, silk and thin serge. If a non-washable fabric was used, women were advised to make a removable lining from cambric or nainsook. The knickers were said to be useful for cycling and boating as well as general wear.

In the hope of resolving the issue I made an appointment at The Clothworkers' Centre for the Study and Conservation of Textiles and Fashion at the Victoria and Albert Museum in London to view a selection of Edwardian underwear. Three pairs of drawers that I viewed in the archive were French-made split drawers with wide, knee-length legs. Each had a deep flounce around the hem with either lace edging and/or lace insertions. One pair, made from fine cotton lawn, had a narrow casing with 32mm wide eau-de-nil satin ribbon threaded through and tied in a bow that sits at the outer edge of the leg. A British-made pair of drawers, dated 1909 and made from wool, was also open between the legs, and so a decision was made to include split drawers in this chapter. While looking at the fabulous collection of underwear in the archive another dilemma arose,

which was the subject of which order the underwear was placed on the body. One set of lingerie had a frill around the hem of the chemise making it unlikely that it would be tucked into a pair of drawers. Fortunately *The Woman's Institute of Domestic Arts & Sciences* lingerie-making booklet provided an answer and suggests that the preference depended on the nationality of the wearer. In France the chemise was worn next to the body whereas American women preferred to wear a knitted vest next to the body. The French chemise was a closer fit and a little shorter while the American chemise was looser and longer and worn over the corset.

SPLIT DRAWERS

The split drawers copied in this chapter are the only project not to be based on a museum garment and were instead bought in an online auction as part of a job lot of assorted vintage clothing. The date is unknown, although they are in keeping with drawers from the late Victorian and early Edwardian period. The owner of the drawers is identified in ink on the outside waistband as G.J. Thomas and a laundry number (c443) appears in faint ink on the inside of the waistband. The edging at the hem is a

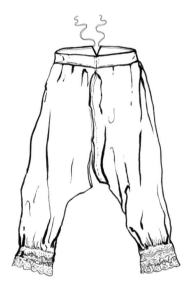

Illustration showing the front view of a pair of split drawers from the author's collection.

particularly fine example of machine-embroidered whitework, or white embroidery on white fabric. The scalloped edge of the frill features a repeating floral design while the band of insertion features a symmetrical wave with small flowers either side. The drawers are tied with long cotton tapes at the centre back. Both museums have

Knee band and frill detail from the original pair of split drawers.

Left: Reproduction split drawers and chemise.

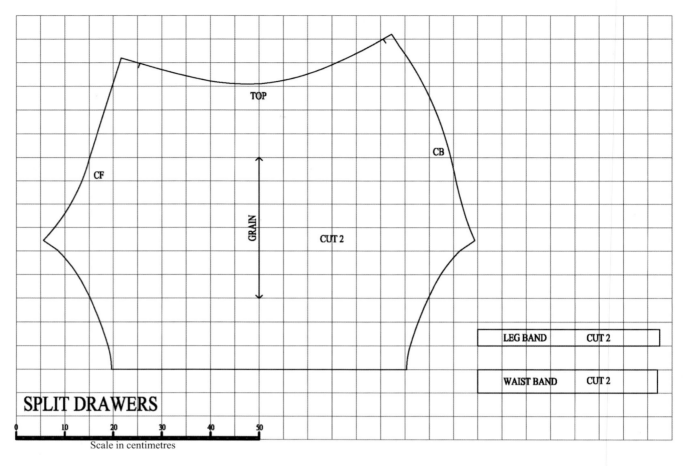

TOP

CB

CF

GRAIN

CUT 2

LEG BAND   CUT 2

WAIST BAND   CUT 2

SPLIT DRAWERS

0   10   20   30   40   50
Scale in centimetres

Split drawers pattern.

MATERIALS AND EQUIPMENT

2 metres medium weight white cotton fabric

Thread

1 metre broderie anglaise insertion lace for the leg bands (optional)

110cm x 1.5cm cotton tape for the waist ties

1.5 metres narrow cotton tape for finishing the inside of the knee bands

120cm scalloped broderie anglaise to edge the legs

Sewing machine

several pairs of drawers but it was difficult to match up the lace or white-work and so this pair has been included as the only non-museum item. Making a pair of drawers was one of the topics covered in *Cutting Out for Student Teachers* written by Amy K. Smith in 1910. The amount of fabric suggested for a pair of drawers was given as 1–2 yards. To make the drawers to the right size readers were advised to take a waist measurement with added ease; this was to be taken without a corset being worn. Comfort was the main concern when making drawers, with plenty of room being left at the knee, as well as the drawers having a wide and deep seat. It was advised that fullness at the waist should be distributed towards the back and a shaped waistband was suggested as being more comfortable than a straight band.

Layout and cutting

Fold the fabric in half lengthways, making sure both selvedges are lined up. Before pinning the pattern in place, make sure it is lying on the straight grain of the fabric. To align the grain line with the straight grain of the fabric, place a pin at one end of the grain symbol and pivot the pattern piece until the line measures equal distances to the folded edge of the fabric. Cut out two legs and two waistband sections. The original drawers have a knee band of white-work or broderie anglaise insertion. I was unable to source a copy of this insertion and so I have cut a band from the white cotton fabric. Add seam allowance to all edges (I added 2cm to all seams and 1cm to the bottom of the leg and to the top of the leg bands). Identify the front of each leg piece; a note with the word 'front' pinned to each section can be useful, especially when attaching the leg bands. It is also worth identifying the centre front and centre back and the top of the legs.

Making order

LEG BANDS

The legs are seamed in one process once the leg band and frill have been sewn to the lower edge. Begin by preparing the frill. Machine two rows of gathering along the top of the broderie anglaise leg trim using a long machine stitch; sew within the seam allowance if possible otherwise the gathering will have to be removed once the frill is attached. To check the length of gathering on the frill, and to distribute the gathers evenly, place a straight rule or flat tape measure on the ironing board and spread the gathers out next to it with the raw edge running alongside the measure, and pin to the board at either end. Once the correct length has been established the loose threads at either end can be secured either by knotting or by wrapping the long threads in a figure of eight around a vertically placed pin at either end. To join the gathered section to the leg band, with right sides facing, line up the raw edges and machine the trim to the band. Trim and press the seam upwards into the band. Gather the bottom of the legs to fit the knee bands. With right sides facing, line up the raw edges and machine the band to the leg and press the seam downwards into the band. Trim the seams to 0.3cm and press lightly, trying not to flatten the gathers. Narrow cotton tape is sewn on top to enclose the seams. Pin the narrow cotton tape on the reverse side to cover all raw edges and topstitch close to the edges along either side. As an alternative a facing made from the same band pattern piece could be hand sewn to the back to enclose the raw edges once the legs are made up, although this adds an extra layer of bulk.

LEGS

The next stage is to make up the legs as two separate cylinders. The edges of the split part of the drawers are finished before joining the lower seams. Fold the edge of the split part of the drawers over by 1cm, press and fold again by a further 1cm and press. Pin in place and topstitch close to the folded edge. The machines used to sew the original drawers would not have had an adjustable stitch length and so the stitches are tiny. A small machine stitch should be used to match the reproduction drawers as closely as possible to the original pair.

Flat felled seams are used to join the inner leg seams on the lower part of the drawers. To make a flat felled seam, with right sides facing line up the raw edges and pin and machine along the seam line. Press the seam allowances to one side. Trim the lower seam down to 0.5cm and the upper seam to 1cm; the seams on the original garment are slightly narrower at 4mm. To complete the flat felled seam, fold the upper seam allowance over the lower trimmed edge and press in place, pin and tack through the centre. Slowly topstitch the seam in place by machining through all layers, sewing close to the folded edge.

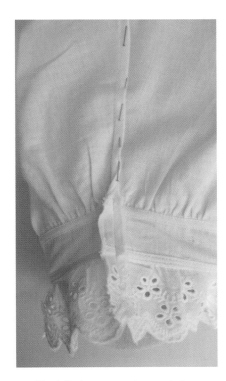

Flat felled seam on the inside leg.

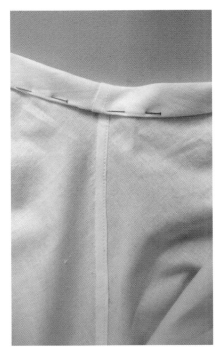

Fold the edge of the upper part of the leg over twice and pin in place.

WAISTBAND

Join the two waistband pieces together down the centre front seams. Trim and press the seam open. Finish the two shorter sides by turning twice and topstitching in place with a narrow hem. Using a long machine stitch, sew two rows of gathering within the seam allowance along the top edge of the drawers, leaving a gap at either edge. The drawers are overlapped at the centre front and secured together before the waistband is attached. With right sides facing place one section on top of the other and overlap by 1cm or the width of your seam allowance, machine across the top and within the seam allowance, to hold in place.

With right sides facing and with the raw edges lined up, working from the right side of the drawers place the top to the front lower edge of the waistband. Pull the gathering stiches until the legs match up with the waistband. (This can also be done by pinning the outer edges of both sections flat to the ironing board.) Distribute the gathers evenly, pin in place and machine along the seam

Detail showing the centre back casings of the drawers.

Illustration of the front view of the chemise from the collection at Royal Pavilion & Museums showing the shape of the tucks and three-dot broderie anglaise trim.

line; press the seam into the waistband. Before the waistband is sewn down a casing needs to be formed for the cotton tapes at the centre back. Press the waistband in half lengthways to mark the top edge of the drawers and then open flat. With the tape running along this line position each tape in 10cm from the finished edge and tack in place. Fold the waistband over and topstitch 9cm in from the edge to hold the tapes in place. Machine a further line of stitching under the tape and 2cm down from the folded edge. To finish the drawers, turn the raw edge of the waistband under so that it sits a fraction below the seam line, and pin and tack in place. Working from the right side of the drawers topstitch close to the bottom edge of the waistband.

CHEMISE

In the Woman's Institute of Domestic Arts & Sciences *Underwear and Lingerie* booklet the chemise is described as a favourite undergarment of many women. The chemise was a roomy garment designed to be tucked into a pair of equally roomy drawers. From observing many variations of the chemise in museum collections I have noticed that the front and back of the garments tend to be the same size, although occasionally the front neck is slightly lower than the back. The chemise was cut on the straight grain and was shaped at the sides. Short

sleeves, if added, were loosely fitted. The front bib area and corresponding back area were gathered or tucked into a band at the neck or yoke. A chemise is finished at the neck, most usually with a straight band and a gathered frill. Some have a placket opening at the front and this also may have a frill inserted around the edge. In *Cutting Out for Student Teachers* Amy K. Smith extols the labour-saving qualities of ready-made trimmings: 'Messrs. J. & J. Cash, of Coventry, prepare various styles of their frilling ready gauged to a feather-stitched band for trimming underwear. This frilling is an immense saving of time.' The shoulders were often placed on a fold and so were straight rather than sloped. Hems on the examples observed were also straight rather than curved. Looking at patterns provided on grids in both *Cutting Out for Student Teachers* (1910) by Amy K. Smith and *How to Make up Garments* (1907) written by Agnes Walker, it can be noted that the reason for the straight shoulders and hems was economy of material – a curved hem would mean wasted fabric. A straight hem would also have been easier for a less experienced dressmaker to make up. The chemise was one of the first things a child learned to make at school. Royal Pavilion & Museums, Brighton & Hove, have a beautifully made, reduced scale chemise made by an eleven-year-old child. The garment was exhibited in the International

Exhibition of 1871 in a section entitled 'Specimens of school-work'. The dressmaking educator Agnes Walker provided instructions for readers to make a chemise by proportion for women and children. For example, to find out the length a measurement should be taken from the top of the shoulder to the length required below the knee.

MATERIALS AND EQUIPMENT

2.10 metres medium weight white cotton fabric

1.70 metres scalloped broderie anglaise to trim the neck and arms

Thread

Ruler or Pattern Master

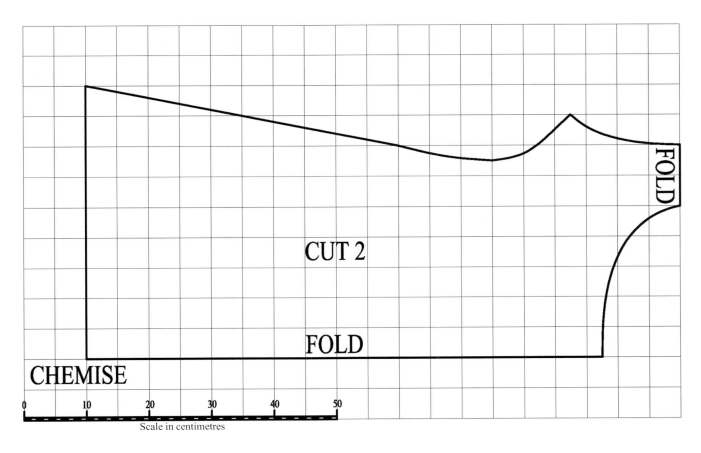

FOLD

CUT 2

FOLD

CHEMISE

0   10   20   30   40   50

Scale in centimetres

Chemise pattern.

The chemise chosen for this project is a white linen chemise from Royal Pavilion & Museums, Brighton & Hove, museum accession number C001011. Made entirely by hand the chemise has slight sleeves trimmed with straight broderie anglaise and a wide round neck finished with a band that is trimmed with straight broderie anglaise. It has sixteen vertical bands of tucking in the front bib area while at the back the fullness is gathered into the neck band. The name 'E. Brown' is handwritten in ink at the centre back neck, which would have identified the garment's owner during the laundering process. Although the museum's chemise is complete and is without repairs, it is stained in places and in need of conservation.

Cutting

This basic chemise pattern can be adapted to fit a range of sizes by varying the number of tucks inserted at the centre front and by dropping the armholes. The back is gathered into a band and so can be adapted to fit the tucks at the front. The tucks are not marked on the pattern but instructions are given for spacing and inserting them. To follow the cutting instructions featured in *Cutting Out for Student Teachers*, fold the fabric in half lengthways and then in half widthways. Place the pattern with the shoulders, centre front and centre back placed against folds. If preferred the fabric can be folded in half lengthways only and an additional seam allowance added to the shoulders. If this method is used then the shoulder seams are joined together with a flat felled seam once the tucks have been inserted in the front and back. Add 1.5cm to all seams; the hem is folded up by 2.5cm with a further 1cm turning and this is included in the pattern, although a longer or shorter length may be preferred. Mark the centre front line with a line of tacking to indicate the desired length of the tucks. Mark the centre back also.

Making order

Begin by making the tucks on the front bib; because the centre front of the bib has a row of tacking already marked at the cutting stage, the edges of each tuck can be measured to radiate out from this line. The number of tucks inserted depends on the size of the wearer. For a size 10–12 chemise insert a total of eighteen tucks, nine either side of the centre front line. These lines form the fold of each tuck. Mark them either with a line of tacking or with an air erasable marker. Using a ruler or a Pattern Master measure straight vertical lines out 2cm both ways from the centre front. Continue to mark at 2cm intervals until a total of eighteen tucks have been marked. The centre four

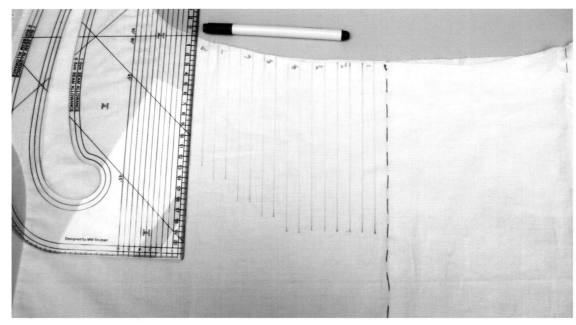

Plot the tucks outwards from the centre front.

tucks measure 16cm in length and the other tucks decrease in size by 1cm so that the final tuck measures 11cm. To mark the tucks press down the centre of each line. Starting from the centre front sew one tuck at a time by machining 0.5cm in from the fold. Press each tuck out of the way before sewing the next one. When all tucks have been sewn press them towards the centre front to match the Royal Pavilion & Museums chemise, or press away from the centre front if preferred.

BACK GATHERS
When the tucks have been inserted measure across the top of the tucked section – this is the measurement to be used for gathering the back neck. To gather along the back neck, set the machine to the longest stitch and sew two parallel lines approximately 0.3cm and 0.6cm apart, close to the seam line. Knot the four threads at one end and pull to gather using the top threads at the other end. Check that the measurement matches the width of the tucks and knot the threads at the other end. Distribute the gathers evenly and using only the tip of the iron, press along the gathers, within the seam allowance.

To make the neck band first join the

short edge with a 1cm seam and press the seam open. The seam of the neckband is positioned at the shoulder rather than the centre front or centre back. Pin the neck band to the chemise with right sides facing. Starting at one shoulder line up the raw edges of the band with the top of the neck and,

working from the chemise side, pin along the neck and machine along the seam line. Press all seams upwards and trim.

Add the broderie anglaise trim to the neckband by placing right sides together, lining up the raw edges and machining within the seam line. Press

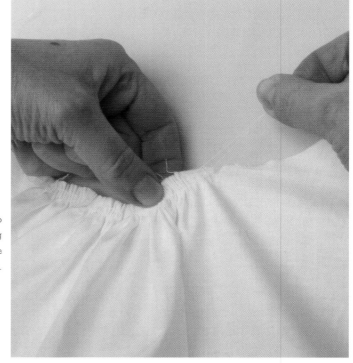

Pull the top two gathering threads at the centre back.

the seams downwards. Take the facing band and press the long edges over by 1cm. Join at the short edge with an open seam and place behind the neck band; pin and tack in place and working from the right side topstitch the facing in place.

To add the broderie anglaise trim to the sleeves place right sides together, lining up the raw edges and machine within the seam line. The join is neatened by a flat felled seam. To create a flat felled seam, with right sides facing line up the raw edges and pin and machine along the seam line; press the seam allowances to one side. Trim the lower seam down to 0.5cm and the upper seam to 1cm. To complete the flat felled seam, fold the upper seam allowance over the lower trimmed edge and press in place, pin and tack through the centre. Slowly topstitch the seam in place by machining through all layers, sewing close to the folded edge.

To finish press the hem over by 1cm and up again by a further 2.5cm. Pin and topstitch the hem by machining close to the folded edge.

ADAPTING THE DRAWERS AND CHEMISE

Royal Pavilion & Museums, Brighton & Hove, have a pair of split drawers that have been altered to form closed drawers. The original stitching has been unpicked but the indented holes from the previous machine stitches are still visible. The new drawers have elastic threaded through the waist. For a quick change in the theatre Velcro could be sewn to the back waist opening of the drawers. The chemise is a really versatile garment that can be adapted in a number of ways. The better quality garments viewed during research were made from the finest, lightweight cottons and had layers of insertion, embroidered names and monograms and narrow ribbons threaded through eyelet ribbon around the neck. The lesser quality garments are made from stiffer cottons – one example could have stood up by itself. The chemise could be altered by adding a placket at the centre front and a single button at the neck edge. The number of tucks could be varied, and the trim. For a quick change in a theatre it would help to cut the armholes looser.

Add the neck band.

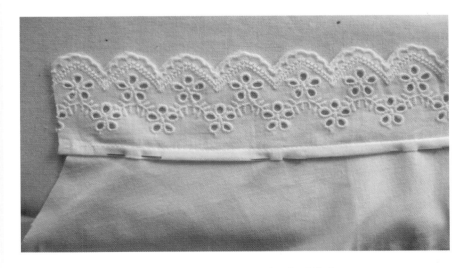

Neaten the edge of the sleeve with a flat felled seam.

Chapter 5
Flounced Petticoat

It is always a mistake to have petticoats long, they so soon get soiled and draggled-looking, if they are. Just to the ankles is the length for a petticoat, not an inch longer – unless, of course, you are the unfortunate possessor of very ugly feet.

The Woman's Institute of Domestic Arts & Sciences booklet *The Dressmaker and Tailor's Shop* advised that it was the duty of a dressmaker to guide the customer to choose the right petticoat: 'Frequently the customer does not realize the importance of securing the right kind of petticoat to wear with a beautiful dress or suit, and it should be the duty of the dressmaker to give her some advice about this matter.' When it came to cutting a petticoat it was suggested that the pattern used for cutting the outside skirt could be used for a petticoat, although the fabric must be suitable. The dressmaker 'should always caution her customer against the wearing of a petticoat that clashes with the outside material or that is too scant or too full for the dress itself, for the petticoat can very easily spoil the effect of an outer garment.'

For evening wear, frilled petticoats were made from 'rustling silk' – this added an auditory element to an evening ensemble. Worthing Museum have a glacé silk petticoat dated 1900–1908; this gored full-length petticoat is fitted at the waist and flares out at the hem. A decorative trim with a serrated edge, also made from glacé silk, has been pleated and sewn to the skirt in a wave around the hem. Taking the petticoat out of its storage box and

Advertisement for a value silk petticoat, the 'Marvel', by Peter Robinson's, Oxford Street, London. Illustrated by Ida Pritchard. (Worthing Museum and Art Gallery)

wrapping of acid-free tissue paper it is striking how much the crunch and rustle of the silk gives an indication of what it must have been like to wear. Frills already constructed with either tucks, pin-tucks, lace insertions or faggoting could be purchased from

haberdashers. In 1902, the weekly trade publication *The Drapers' Record* featured an advertisement listing twelve types of ready-made frilling for sewing onto underwear, which was said to be a way of saving both time and money, and also of avoiding the

Left: Reproduction petticoat.

Illustration of the original petticoat from the collection at Royal Pavilion & Museums, Brighton & Hove.

Eau-de-nil satin ribbon threaded through wide eyelet lace around the skirt of a satin and tulle petticoat. (Worthing Museum and Art Gallery)

'vexatious' activity of making frills. The demise of the full frilled petticoat came with the rise in popularity of the new Empire-line silhouette, although the petticoat was still decorative and considered a vital garment. In 1912 Peter Robinson's in the West End of London were advertising a slim-line petticoat called 'The Marvel', which was sketched for the advertisement by fashion illustrator Ida Pritchard. The peach-coloured petticoat was made from silk taffeta and was finished at the hem with a deep flounce of box pleats. It was also available in a wide range of colours including ivory, turquoise, pink, pale blue, grey, light brown, dark brown, red, navy, light navy, black, and white.

The petticoat featured in this chapter is from the collection at Royal Pavilion & Museums, Brighton & Hove, museum accession number H56/21/69. It is completely sewn by hand with tiny stitches, a fact that only became obvious when photographs taken in the archive were enlarged on the computer. Although the petticoat is not dated it resembles petticoats featured in advertisements from 1906 to 1908. The petticoat is formed of a main full-length skirt with an additional flounce sewn on top halfway down. The main petticoat is made from white cotton and it is shaped to fit the body with five gored panels. The centre front panel drops in a slight curve at the waist; it has a vertical buttonhole at the centre front, which was possibly used to fasten the petticoat to another garment. The name 'Adrienne' is embroidered in delicate satin stitch to one side of the buttonhole. The petticoat is flat at the front and smooth over the hips, a small amount of fullness is gathered at the centre back in small pleats and it can be pulled in and gathered further when tied. Ties made from cotton tape are threaded through two small channels at the centre back. The ties are long enough to tie once at the back and bring around to the centre front to tie in a bow. Three different laundry markings are crudely sewn in red and blue thread at the back waist.

The outer flounced layer of the petticoat hangs off a straight piece of crocheted eyelet lace that would originally have had a ribbon threaded through and tied in a bow at one side – this is now missing. The ribbon would have been removed for laundering and kept separately and perhaps it was never replaced after its last wash. Petticoats from a similar date in Worthing Museum and The Clothworkers' Centre for the Study and Conservation of Textiles and Fashion have eau-de-nil or pale blue ribbon threaded though eyelet lace. A piece of cotton tape with round, flat, fabric-covered weights attached at intervals

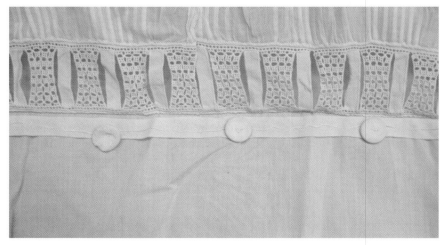

Detail showing a band of weighted cotton tape sewn behind the eyelet lace of the original petticoat.

Detail showing layers of lace in the outer flounce of the original petticoat.

4 metres white medium weight cotton for the main petticoat

4 metres white lightweight cotton for the flounce

12 x 4.5cm metres insertion lace

Eyelet lace and satin ribbon (optional)

1.80 metres crocheted eyelet lace or straight cotton lace, 1.5–3cm wide

3 metres x 1cm wide picot edging lace

1.60 metres x 12mm white cotton tape

Thread

Cutting

PETTICOAT AND FRILL

The petticoat should be cut out by following the grain lines on the pattern. 1.5cm seam allowance should be added to the top and sides with 6cm added to the hem. To face the waistband a bias strip measuring 80cm x 5cm is needed, which includes seam allowance. The lower frill is cut along the selvedge and measures 8cm x 3 metres, which also includes seam allowance. Thread mark the position of the flounce with tailor's tacks.

SEPARATE FLOUNCE

The top flounce is 4 metres x 36cm when finished, with a lower frill, which is sewn to the edge of the flounce, measuring 4.5 metres x 10cm when finished. To make the flounce, join widths of fabric together with tiny French seams to make a 4-metre length, or cut a straight piece along the selvedge. A less full flounce can be made if the maker would rather not sew so many pin-tucks in the upper layer. Three strips of insertion lace measuring 4 metres each, and one piece of

runs behind the eyelet lace. This would have prevented the lightweight and very full petticoat from riding up.

The layer of lightweight cotton fabric sewn to the bottom of the eyelet lace is comprised of rows of vertical pin-tucks. There are three lace insertions below this, each 4.5cm wide, which are inserted in stripes around the outer layer. A useful guide to identifying the lace used on petticoats is lace expert Pat Earnshaw's book *A Dictionary of Lace*. The lace on the museum's petticoat appears to be 'Valenciennes', which by the Victorian period was being produced in France and Belgium and is described as 'a neat durable lace used for undergarments' favoured by European aristocracy. Valenciennes can

be recognized by its diamond-shaped mesh and curving patterns of flowers and fronds. Valenciennes lace was a popular trim for undergarments and it was often mentioned in society journal *The Ladies' Field* and the French fashion journal *La Mode Illustrée*. Having established that the petticoat was beautifully crafted and made from expensive lace it perhaps comes as no surprise to find a darned section at the back of the hem – perhaps this is where the heel of a shoe caught the edge of the flounce. With so much care and attention going into the making of the petticoat it was obviously not going to be discarded just for the sake of a small hole.

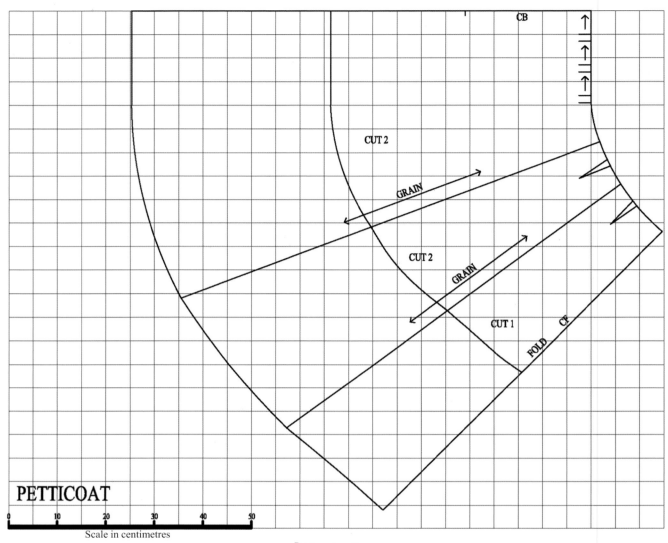

PETTICOAT

0   10   20   30   40   50

Scale in centimetres

Petticoat pattern.

crocheted eyelet lace, or straight cotton lace are also needed.

Making order

Begin by making the darts in the front panels. Working on the wrong side of the fabric fold the dart down the centre, pin in place and machine from the wide end to the point. Each dart is 7cm long and is pressed towards the centre front when completed. The next stage is to join the seams. On the original petticoat a tiny 3mm French seam is used. To make a French seam place wrong sides together and machine so that the raw edges show on the right

side of the petticoat. Trim the seam allowance away close to the line of stitching and, to replicate the original seam, trim the seam down to 2mm. Press the seam to one side and then fold along the seam from the right side with the raw edges enclosed inside. Pin and machine a 3mm seam. Press the French seams away from the centre front. The centre back also has a French seam up to the opening. The centre back opening can be finished off by turning the fabric over twice and topstitching in place.

Form the pleats at the centre back following the directional arrows on the pattern. To finish the raw edges at the

top of the petticoat, a facing cut on the bias is sewn along the inside of the waist. A space is left open in the back panels only to form a casing, which a cotton tape passes through in order to gather the waist in to fit the wearer. To make the facing, fold the bias strip in half lengthways and press; measure against the top of the petticoat to check the length and machine down the inside of both short edges. Turn the right way round and press. Place the strip along the outside of the waist with the raw edges lining up. Machine along the seam line and trim and layer the seam to eliminate as much bulk as possible. Fold the facing to the inside

The position of the pleats at the centre back of the petticoat.

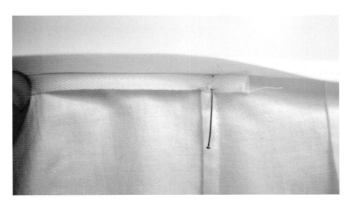

The position of the cotton ties at the back waist, which are sewn to the seam and then encased in the facing.

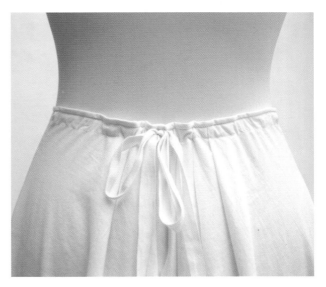

Back detail of the finished petticoat.

Adding a frill to the lower edge of the main petticoat.

of the petticoat leaving a 2mm line of facing showing on the right side. Pin in place and sink stitch to form a line of narrow piping. Before machining the bottom edge of the facing, pin the cotton tapes to the side back seams and then machine to the seam allowance. Keep the tapes out of the way and pin and machine along the bottom of the facing, sewing close to the fold. To finish the hem of the petticoat press the

hem over by 1cm and up again by a further 5cm. Pin and topstitch the hem by machining close to the folded edge.

FRILL

Frills are applied to Edwardian underwear using two methods: the first is to place two rolled edges together and to overstitch by hand using small stitches that at times are barely visible to the eye. The second method is to sew

a frill upside down and then press it downwards. This is the method used to sew the bottom frill to the reproduction petticoat.

To make the frill, machine the straight edge of the picot lace on top of the selvedge. Join the ends of the frill with a French seam and press to one side. Mark the frill into four sections and using the longest machine stitch sew a double row of gathering in each of the four sections. Mark the hem into four corresponding sections. Pull the gathering threads until the frill fits the petticoat and secure the ends of the gathers. Press the gathers along the raw edge, pressing within the seam allowance and using the tip of the iron

Detail of pin-tucks
in the flounce of
the original
petticoat.

Inserting lace in the flounce.

only. Place the frill upside down around the outside of the hem, with right sides facing and the raw edge of the frill butting up against the row of machining holding the hem in place. Pin the frill in place, distributing the gathers evenly as you go. Machine the frill to the petticoat, trim all threads and smooth the frill downwards and press lightly along the top of the frill.

TOP FLOUNCE

If using the width of the fabric, join sections together using narrow French seams. Leave the centre back seam open at this stage. To make up the top layer of the petticoat, begin by making

the pin-tucks in a length of fine muslin. A pin-tuck foot and a twin needle can be used to make this process easier; you will also need two reels of thread. The pin-tucks on the original petticoat are 2mm wide and are sewn in vertical bands around the top layer. Each band is comprised of seven pin-tucks which are all 12.5cm long and when sewn they measure 4cm across. A 4cm gap is left before sewing the next band of pin-tucks and this is repeated all around the top layer. The band is 16cm long and so the space below the pin-tucks flares out allows the layer below to be cut from a longer piece of fabric.

The first layer of the reproduction

petticoat is also 16cm long and has just two pin-tucks which are 12cm long, sewn every 6cm. On the original petticoat the layer below the pin-tucks is a row of lace followed by a layer of muslin; this is repeated until three layers of lace are inserted. The final layer of the flounce is a frill edged with a delicate picot lace if this can be sourced; an alternative is to use a machine embroidery finish. The top layer of pin-tucks is joined to the petticoat with a row of eyelet lace, which would have been threaded with satin ribbon.

The reproduction petticoat has two rows of insertion lace. The first is sewn to the bottom of the pin-tucked section by placing the lace on the right side, along the bottom of the pin-tucked section with a 1cm overlap. Pin the lace in place and machine along the edge of the lace. The other layers of fabric and lace are sewn by the same method. To neaten the fabric behind the lace roll over twice and topstitch through all layers or trim the raw edge down to 0.5cm and let the raw seam allowance

To make a simpler petticoat
suitable for a woman on a lesser
income the top flounce of lace
insertions and pin-tucks can be
omitted. A final row of running
stitch can be sewn 1cm down from
the top of the frill; this will secure
the frill in place. Many cheaper
petticoats have a frill sewn using
the same method as the frill sewn
around the bottom of this
petticoat. Alternatively the flounce
can be reduced in width and
made without the lace insertions.
If a fuller petticoat with extra
volume is required, the width of
the flounce, before gathering onto
the crocheted band, can be
increased. An additional layer of
flounce can also be added
underneath to increase the width
of the hem of a skirt.

Preparing the
frill to sew
around the
edge of the
flounce.

sit behind the lace.

To finish the flounce a layer of cotton
lace is sewn on top of the pin-tucked
layer. Place the top edge of cotton lace
along the flounce position thread
marked line traced, and pin and tack. If

possible, check the length is even all
around by placing on a dress stand
before machining the lace in place,
sewing close to the top edge. The lower
frill around the bottom of the flounce is

made in the same way as the previous
frill, although the bottom edge has
been neatened by turning twice and
using a decorative stitch on the sewing
machine that forms small scallops.

Chapter 6
Blouse with Tucks and Lace Insertions

The Morning Leader printed an article in 1907 concerning two sisters described as 'decayed gentlewomen'. Having fallen on hard times the two women applied for blouse-making outwork at a Regent Street warehouse. Fabric was supplied, but barely enough to do the job and so cutting out the blouse was 'a horrible sort of nightmare'. The article explains, the blouse had 'hundreds of little pin-tucks' and was the sisters' own design. They worked together all one evening and then all day and late into the next evening to sew the blouse. They had to use their own buttons, sewing silk and ribbons, which was something most dressmakers would have been expected to do. The shop was said to have been delighted with the finished result. From the initial conversation at the warehouse the women had expected to be paid eight shillings and six pence but in fact were paid just six shillings between them. This was a common practice for home dressmakers, who were not covered by employment laws. The disturbing conclusion to the story is that two days later the blouse was displayed in the shop window of the establishment, fraudulently advertised as 'The Latest From Paris' with a price of six and a half guineas, a handsome profit for the unscrupulous warehouse.

The blouse featured in this chapter is from Worthing Museum, museum accession number 54/529. At first glance this might look like a difficult project to reproduce but it is actually a basic shape and all pin-tucks and lace sections are made separately and then sewn on top of each other using the pattern as a template. The original blouse is entirely sewn by hand with small, neat and regular stitching, which was obviously carried out by a skilled maker. The blouse has a small square woven label at the centre back waist. The red number 36 indicates the bust size and careful measuring of the garment verifies this to be the case. A size label suggests that the blouse was made to be sold in a department store or small shop, rather than it being a garment made for an individual customer. This makes the fact that it was hand sewn all the more remarkable. Hopefully the maker of this blouse fared better with her employer

Lace blouse with three-quarter-length sleeves, high neck and pouched bodice sketched by fashion illustrator Ida Pritchard, c.1906. (Worthing Museum and Art Gallery)

Left: The reproduction blouse mounted on a black dress stand.

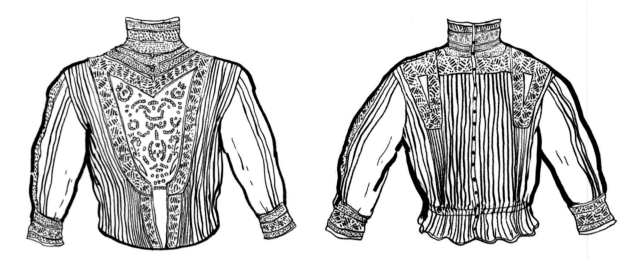

Front and back view illustrations of the original blouse from Worthing Museum and Art Gallery.

than the sisters described in *The Morning Leader* article.

The blouse is made from fine white cotton with decorative tucks, pin-tucks and lace insertions. It has a centre front panel of hand-embroidered cut work that is edged with a wide lace insertion. It has a boned collar made from straight lengths of lace, and is bound at the top edge with a narrow strip of cotton fabric. The three-quarter-length sleeves have two rows of insertion lace running down the centre of the sleeves, which sit either side of a hand-embroidered panel with cut work. There are three sets of tucks at either side of the insertions. The sleeves are finished with cuffs made from three straight pieces of lace joined together in the same way as the collar; the cuffs are also finished with a narrow binding of cotton fabric. The front of the blouse is longer than the back to allow the front to create a pouched effect. The blouse fastens at the centre back with metal snap fasteners and two shirt buttons and hand-worked loops on the collar. It would have been extremely difficult for a woman to get dressed in this blouse without help. A lady's maid would have been needed to close the fastenings.

CUTTING

Cutting and making this blouse is a bit like doing a jigsaw puzzle: it builds up one piece at a time. All of the tucked sections are straight pieces of fabric that are shaped to the pattern once the tucks have been sewn in place. The central panel forms the template for a layer of insertion lace that is sewn around it. This means that the basic pattern cannot be used to cut out any sections until the decorative pieces are formed and assembled. It also means that there is an element of artistic licence in assembling the blouse and additional insertions of lace can be added if required.

The first section to prepare for cutting is the centre front panel. Mark the straight grain of the centre of the embroidered panel with a row of tacking, and then centre the template over the panel. Pin in place and tack carefully around the edge. Add 1.5cm seam allowance all around and cut out. The sleeves can be left plain and cut from the fabric or they can have rows of insertion lace added down the centre. The completed section is placed on top of the pattern and the outline is traced with thread marking. A seam allowance of 1.5cm is added before cutting out. The lengths of lace for the collar and

MATERIALS AND EQUIPMENT

2 metres white cotton voile

5 metres x 3.5cm crocheted lace insertion or straight edged cotton lace with an open weave

2.5 metres x 2cm straight edged cotton lace with an open weave

Centre front cut work embroidered panel

2 mother-of-pearl flat shirt buttons

50cm plastic boning (such as Rigelene) for the collar

15 metal snap fasteners

Austrian cotton faggoting (optional)

Sewing machine with pin-tuck foot

Double sewing machine needle

2 reels of white thread

Dress stand

Pattern Master

Air erasable marker

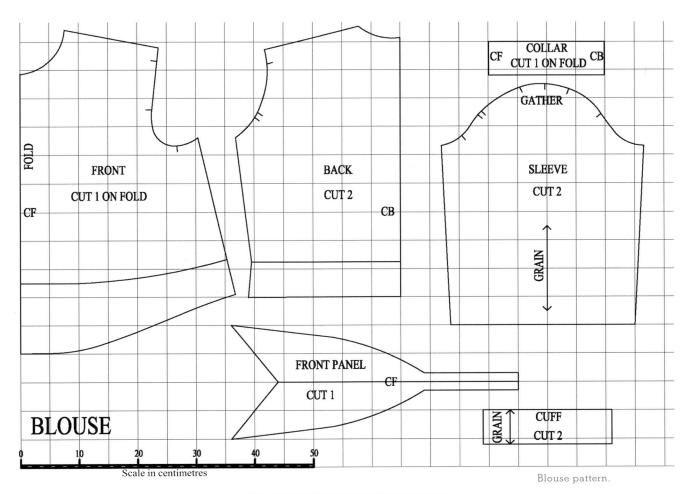

FOLD

CF

FRONT
CUT 1 ON FOLD

BACK
CUT 2

CB

SLEEVE
CUT 2

GRAIN

CF COLLAR CB
CUT 1 ON FOLD

GATHER

FRONT PANEL

CF

CUT 1

GRAIN CUFF
CUT 2

BLOUSE

0   10   20   30   40   50

Scale in centimetres

Blouse pattern.

The front panel marked out with pins and
the first layer of lace sewn down the
sides.

cuffs can be cut by using the pattern
pieces as a guide.

Making order
FRONT PANEL

Insertion lace was extremely popular in
the Edwardian era; it does not enjoy the
same popularity now and therefore is
difficult to source. I discovered some
handmade scalloped edge lace in a
similar pattern in an antique shop. I
washed the lace and placed the
scallops so that one edge sat on top of
the other. Once the scallops had been
zigzagged together and pressed flat
they made a good wide insertion lace.
A further difficulty was the hand-
embroidered panel. To recreate this
effect I have used an embroidered table
runner from the same period. Many
small cloths and runners are still in
existence in antique and vintage shops.

Once the panel has been thread
marked and cut using the template, cut
the lace insertions that outline the
centre panel leaving enough seam
allowance on the end of each piece for
joining. Pin the lace insertion on top of
the front panel all around the edge,
with the edge of the lace sitting
alongside the tacking. Topstitch close
to the edge nearest to the front panel.

Turn the panel the wrong way round
and using the Pattern Master and an air
erasable marker, mark 1cm away from
the stitching. Cut along this line and
then press the edge over by 0.5cm.
Press again until all raw edges are
neatened, pin and tack in place and
slipstitch along the folded edge. The
insertions on the original blouse are
joined by hand using an overstitching
or overcasting method.

The front neck is filled in with three
straight rows of insertion lace that are

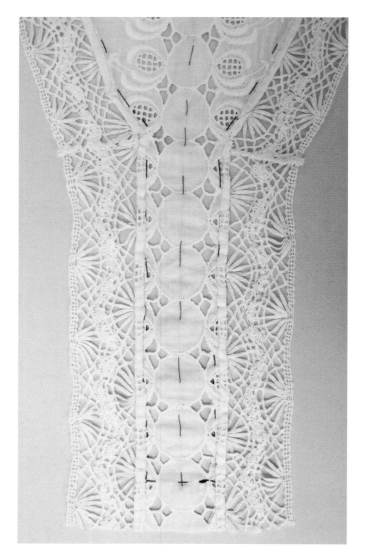

Back view of the front panel showing how to neaten the front panel by folding the seam allowance twice and slipstitching along the fold.

Back view detail of the front panel showing where to form a dart in each layer of lace sewn above the front panel before adding the next layer.

shaped into a V at the front neck by forming a dart on the reverse. Each layer is attached separately and the dart made before moving onto the next layer. To add the first layer take a straight piece of lace and pin it slightly under the top lace attached to the front panel. Make sure the centre will pattern match when made into a dart. Machine the lace in place by topstitching and press. To form the dart lay the section face down on a flat surface and pinch the excess lace into a dart. I found it easier to sew the dart by hand because it makes it easier to control the matching of the pattern. Repeat this

process until all three layers are in lace, making sure that the pattern in each layer mirrors the pattern in the layer below.

PIN-TUCKS AND TUCKS

Add a pin-tuck foot and double needle to the sewing machine and follow any guidelines in your machine instructions for stitch length and tension. I used a small stitch and did not adjust the tension. Thread the machine with two reels of thread, one passing through each needle. It is advisable to make a sample before attempting to sew pin-tucks on the

blouse.

To make the side bodice sections cut a square of fabric 80cm x 80cm. Use the completed front panel as a guide to mark a curved line to show the position of the pin-tucks, although it is a good idea to continue sewing the tucks 2cm up beyond this line to allow for any movement in the fabric. Measure 6cm in from the selvedge and draw the first line with an air erasable marker. Using the guide of the pin-tuck foot, machine the first row of pin-tucks. Each line after this should use the groove of the foot as a guide to follow the previous pin-tuck. Press lightly once all pin-tucks are sewn

Add a double needle and pin-tuck foot to the machine and begin sewing the pin-tucks.

Use a single needle and the usual machine foot to sew rows of tucks alongside the pin-tucks.

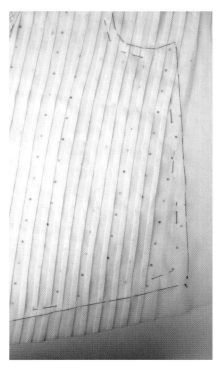

Thread mark around the edge of the pattern to show the seam lines and add seam allowance.

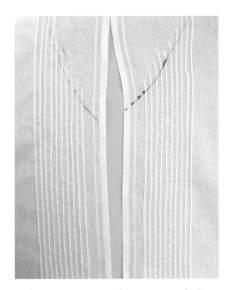

Completed pin-tuck sections with the position of the front panel marked with the purple lines of an air erasable marker.

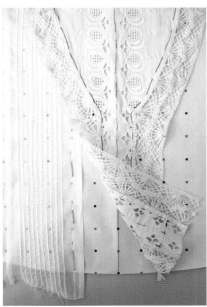

To join the front panel to the side panels, place the tucked sections on top of the pattern, lay the front panel on top and pin together.

and pull the fabric back into shape.

To sew the tucks, replace the pin-tuck foot with the usual machine foot and remove the double needle and replace with a single needle. Use an air erasable marker to mark a straight line alongside the last pin-tuck. The line should be 1.5cm away from the pin-tuck. Mark 14 further lines 2.5cm apart. To sew the first tuck, fold along the line and press; the tuck is machined 0.5cm in from the folded edge. Continue machining one tuck at a time until all tucks are sewn in place and then press away from the centre front. Use the pattern as a template to place the lace panel over the tucked section. To cut out the shape of the blouse place it over the pattern and thread mark around the edge. The back panels have vertical rows of tucks with a section of pin-tucks in the centre. Above the pin-tucks there is an insertion of lace.

SEAMS

The side seams are offset and sit towards the back of the blouse. The seam is joined together with a

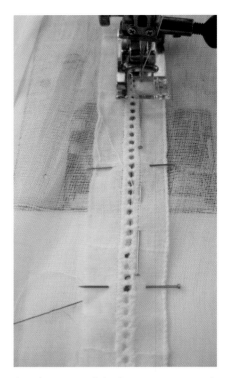

Lay the centre of the faggoting on top of the seam line and machine down the right side.

readymade insertion of Austrian faggoting. Place the faggoting with right sides facing on top of the thread marked seam line. Machine close to the right side of the faggoting and then trim the blouse seam down to 0.5cm. Pin and topstitch the blouse to the outer edge of the faggoting trim and press. On the original blouse the seams have been rolled and overcast. The armholes in the original garment feature an insertion of cotton faggoting which has not been added to the reproduction.

There is no shoulder seam on the original blouse. The front and back sections are joined at the shoulders either side of a row of 3.5cm insertion lace.

CENTRE BACK FASTENING

The original blouse fastens down the centre back with 15 metal snap fasteners which are fixed onto strips of satin ribbon. This was a readymade closure which is no longer produced. A contemporary substitute is readymade plastic snap fasteners attached to cotton tape; alternatively, individual press studs can be sewn to satin ribbon or cotton tape.

SLEEVES

The sleeves on the original blouse have two rows of insertion lace down the centre of a hand-embroidered panel; this can be achieved by using the pattern as a template. The reproduction blouse has one layer of 3.5cm insertion lace. To add one layer of lace, cut the lace to the length of the sleeve. Tack a straight line from the tip of the sleeve head to the bottom edge of the sleeve. Centre the lace along the line and topstitch close to the edge of the lace. On the wrong side cut up the centre of the fabric under the lace and roll the seam allowances over and pin in place and either slipstitch by hand or topstitch through all layers. To add tucks either side of the insertion lace in the sleeves, cut straight pieces of fabric measuring 45cm long and 22cm wide. Mark three tucks down the length of the fabric, each 2.5cm apart. The tucks are then machined in place by sewing 0.5cm in from the fold. The insertion lace should then be added and the tucks pressed away from the lace. Place the newly assembled panel over the sleeve pattern and thread mark around the edge of the sleeve and add a 1.5cm seam allowance. Before inserting the sleeve, using a long stitch, machine and sew two rows of gathers between the balance marks along the sleeve head and along the bottom of the sleeve, within the seam allowance. To insert the sleeves, with right sides facing, match up the balance marks and pin and machine in place. The seams can be trimmed and either overlocked together or rolled and overcast.

CUFFS

The cuffs are formed from three layers of straight lace joined together, laying the two outer layers over the wider inner layer. The lace is joined by machining the layers together with a straight stitch. There is no opening in the cuffs; they should be loose enough to pass over the hand. A cotton binding finishes off the edge of the original cuff although this has been left off the reproduction blouse. To add a binding cut a strip on the straight grain and place against the outside of the cuff. With the edges lined up, machine a narrow seam. Fold the binding to the reverse side of the cuff and fold twice to neaten before slipstitching in place. When the cuffs have been added the sleeves can be joined using a French seam.

COLLAR

The collar is formed from three straight rows of cotton lace using the same method as the cuffs. The original lace may have been crocheted. The open weave of the lace allows the collar to stretch and mould to the shape of the neck. In total the original collar is 7cm deep which includes the flat binding along the top. The collar fastens with two flat mother-of-pearl buttons and two hand-worked loops at the centre back. There are two sections of collar boning positioned at angles to the centre front. The boning feels like steel rods and is covered in white satin fabric and has flossing at the top and

Place the blouse on a stand and pin the collar around the neck.

bottom. The satin is machined down the sides and given that this is a handmade blouse, indicates that the boning was purchased readymade. A reproduction set of boning can be made by covering plastic boning with readymade satin bias binding. Because of the way the blouse has been constructed the neck edge is not rounded and so it is easier to judge the position of the collar by placing the blouse on a dress stand. Mark the centre front of the collar and line it up with the centre front of the neck. The collar sits on top of the blouse and once pinned in place is sewn on by hand.

ADAPTING THE BLOUSE

The basic blouse shape can be used for a simpler version although even the simplest of blouses had some form of decoration, for example blouses at the cheaper end of the market had the insertion lace sewn on top of the fabric. For a blouse suitable for a woman on a lower income in the Edwardian period the basic blouse shape could be made using a small floral print fabric. Snap fasteners are useful for a quick change and could be used instead of buttons on the collar; alternatively, circles of Velcro could be sewn down the centre back.

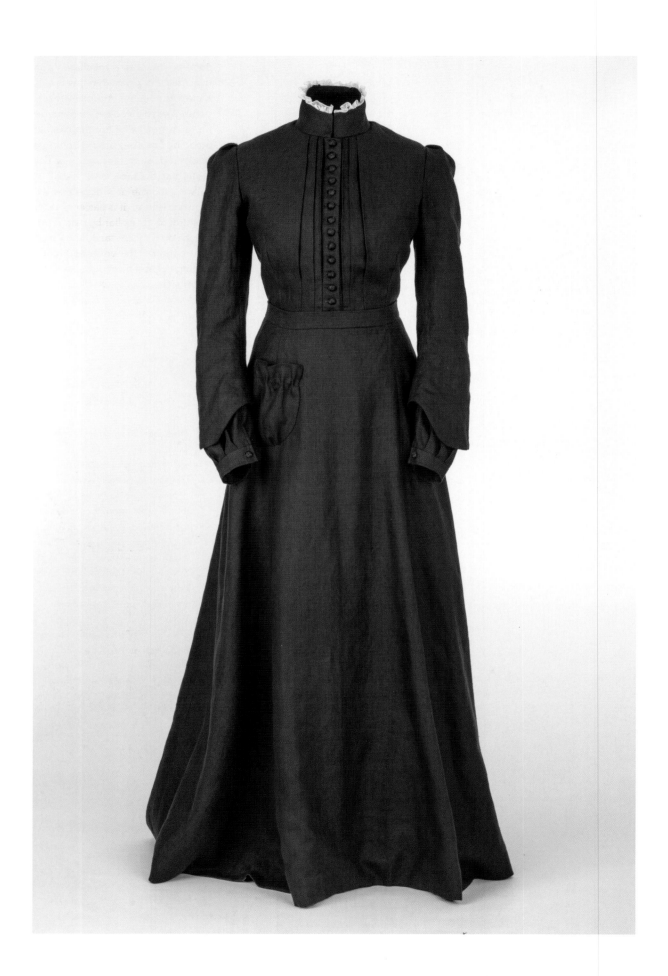

Chapter 7
Two-Part Walking Dress

The plain skirt and bodice, also known as a tailor-made costume, was a useful and versatile element of the Edwardian woman's wardrobe. The skirt could also be worn separately with a blouse. In 1900 'Madame Modish' wrote in The Lady's World *of the practicalities of a plain skirt: 'we...find it very convenient to have our skirts adorned without introducing a foreign element that might quarrel with one blouse while it fraternised with another.' The walking dress chosen for this chapter comes from Worthing Museum and dates from c.1901, museum accession number 1962/1627/1&2. It is made from a loose-weave grey wool, which is mounted onto Silesia. Curator Gerry Connolly suggests that this walking dress is the type of outfit worn by a governess, and it has many features which support this idea. It is a practical and plain outfit but has many delightful details. The bodice is fastened down the centre front with fifteen small black flower-shaped shank buttons. There are two further buttons, one on each cuff. It has a straight stand collar that is trimmed on the inside with a band of gathered ivory lace that has been loosely hand stitched, indicating that it was removed for laundering. The sleeves have a false cuff sitting under a sleeve which flares out at the lower edge. The bodice is fitted to the body and has pleats either side of the centre front and three sets of tucks machined in place either side of the centre back.*

Around the waistline of the bodice are four evenly spaced flat buttons used for fastening the bodice to the skirt. The waistband of the skirt has four horizontal buttonholes and a cross, stitched in red thread at the centre front, making it likely that a belt would have been worn on top to hide these details. The skirt is comprised of five gored panels with a centre back,

Front and back detail of the walking dress.

placket opening. It has three useful pockets including a decorative front patch pocket, which is well constructed and hand sewn to the skirt with two rows of stitching and so would have been strong and functional. A tiny square pocket is sewn at the front of the inside of the waistband, which might have been used for a watch. The final pocket is concealed in a back pleat and the purpose of such a pocket was explained by Cynthia Asquith in her memoirs, *Remember and Be Glad.* Reflecting on herself as a seventeen-year-old debutante in 1904, she did not recall when she first carried a handbag, rather she used a 'placket-hole' pocket

MATERIALS AND EQUIPMENT

5 metres grey loose weave wool
3 metres Silesia or similar cotton for mounting the skirt
2 metres striped cotton lining for mounting the bodice
2 skirt hooks and bars
4 snap fasteners
Collar canvas
Thread
17 small shank buttons
Petersham for the waistband
Sewing machine

Left: The reproduction two-part walking dress.

in her skirts for carrying a leather partitioned purse and a handkerchief. This is the only example of a plain wool skirt that I could find in either museum. One explanation might be that skirts were made from large pieces of fabric and therefore could have been unpicked and remodelled at a later stage. There are many examples of decorative skirts at both museums. Royal Pavilion & Museums have a gored skirt in a wide black-and-white stripe with a flounce at the hem topped with a broad zigzag of black braid. Worthing Museum even has a collection of simple lightweight striped summer skirts still bearing the shop label and prices. A medium-weight linen has been used for the reproduction dress, which has a similar weave to the original wool and is a close colour match, although if a similar wool fabric can be sourced this would be a better fabric for a costume due to the creasing properties of linen. The skirt is mounted with black cotton and the bodice with a striped grey and cream vintage cotton lining fabric. Cutting and making instructions have been given separately for the skirt and bodice in case readers prefer to make only the skirt. In each case enlarge the pattern, add seam allowance and use it to cut and make a toile to test the shape and fit of the dress before cutting in fabric.

SKIRT

Cutting and mounting

Begin by cutting the mounting sections. Press the fabric, fold in half and lay the skirt pattern pieces on the mounting fabric by following the grain lines on the pattern pieces. Pin in place and use tailor's chalk with a sharpened edge to draw around the edge of the pattern; add seam allowance and cut out. Remove the pattern pieces and use carbon paper and a tracing wheel to transfer the tailor's chalk pattern markings to the under piece of mounting fabric.

Press the skirt fabric, and, if using

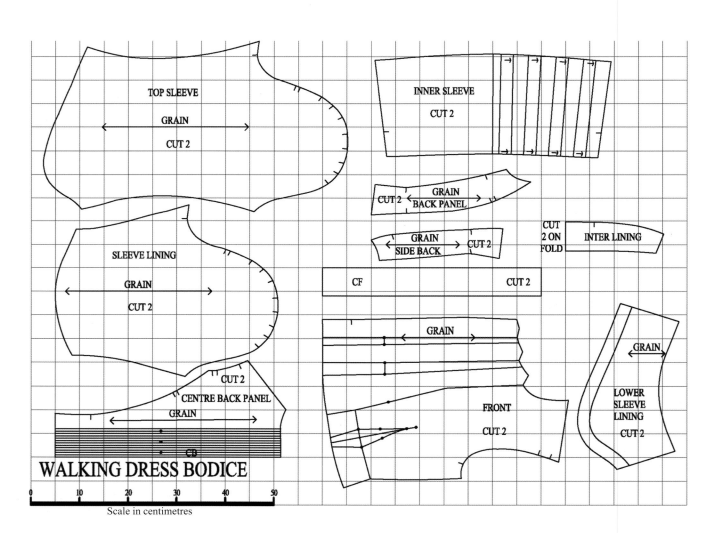

Walking dress pattern A.

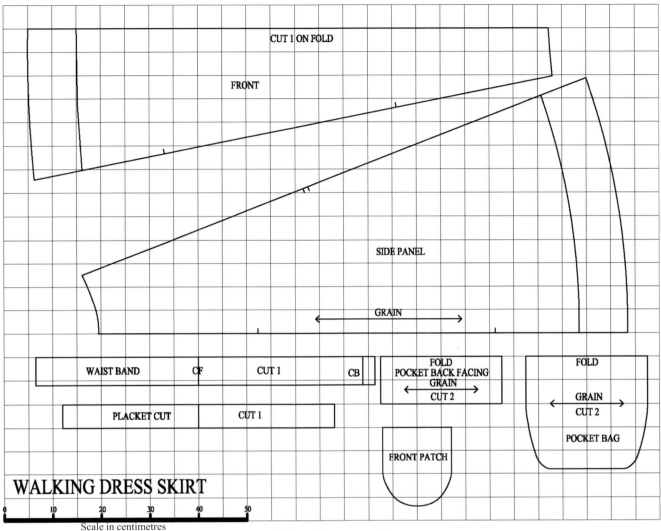

CUT 1 ON FOLD

FRONT

SIDE PANEL

GRAIN

WAIST BAND   CF   CUT 1   CB

FOLD
POCKET BACK FACING
GRAIN
CUT 2

FOLD

GRAIN
CUT 2

POCKET BAG

PLACKET CUT   CUT 1

FRONT PATCH

WALKING DRESS SKIRT

0   10   20   30   40   50

Scale in centimetres

Walking dress pattern B.

wool, shrink the fabric by hovering the steam iron close to the surface and then allowing to dry. Fold the fabric in half lengthways with right sides together and the selvedges matching, and place all pattern pieces on the fabric with the grain lines following the straight grain of the fabric. Pin in place and add a generous seam allowance of at least 3cm all around and cut. Remove the pattern pieces from the fabric. Separate the skirt pieces and lay each one flat on the cutting table with the wrong side facing upwards.

The original placket hole pocket is not reinforced with interfacing but this is something to consider at this stage. A rectangle of fusible interfacing can be placed over the pocket opening on the reverse side of the fabric before mounting takes place.

Place the corresponding mounting fabric piece on top of the skirt fabric piece with the pattern markings facing upwards. Pin in place, taking care to smooth both layers until flat. Using a single thread, tack along the pattern lines through both layers. Make sure the top corners of each skirt piece are clearly marked on the right sides. Also thread mark the placket opening, balance points and pleats in the two back pieces. Use the hem facing marked along the bottom of the skirt

pattern to cut the hem facing pieces from the skirt fabric; add seam allowance.

Making order
PLACKET HOLE POCKET

According to *Weldon's Home Dressmaker* the placket hole pocket must always be positioned on the left-hand side of the back of the skirt. This is most likely because it was easier to reach with the right hand. It is easier to make the placket hole pocket before the skirt is sewn together.

The pocket bag is a long rectangular shape with rounded edges. Place the

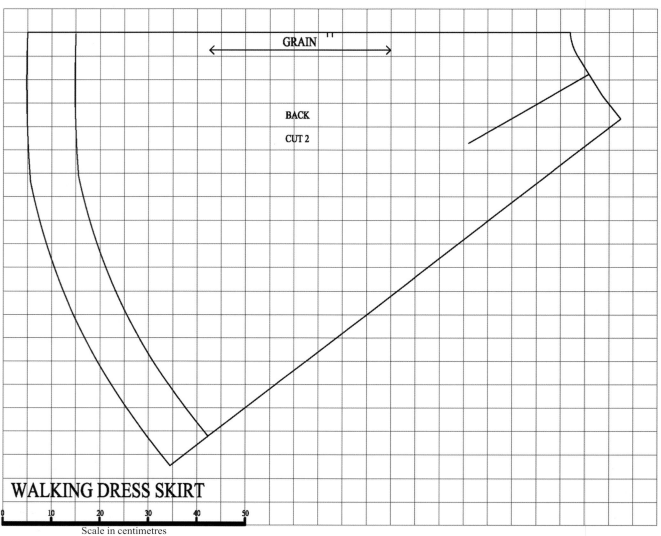

GRAIN

BACK

CUT 2

WALKING DRESS SKIRT

0   10   20   30   40   50

Scale in centimetres

Walking dress pattern C.

pocket facing over the centre of the pocket bag, turn the edges of the facing under and topstitch along the folded edge of the facing. Mark the centre of the pocket from the top to the bottom of the short edge of the bag with a row of tacking. Before attaching the pocket, machine an elliptical shape around the opening on the skirt using a small machine stitch; this will help to reinforce the pocket opening. Working from the right side of the skirt, place the pocket bag over the opening with the right side facing upwards. Pin in place and working from the inside of the skirt tack a line through all layers to show the position of the elliptical line

of reinforced stitching. Turn the skirt with the right side facing you and machine just slightly outside of this line. The opening now needs to be cut open using small, sharp scissors. It is a good idea to start in the centre and cut out towards each edge – this minimizes the risk of cutting through the stitching.

The pocket bag is joined together using a French seam, which sits on the outside when finished. To join the pocket bag place right sides together and pin around the edge. Machine along the seam line and trim the seam allowance down to 0.5cm. Clip into the seam at the rounded corners and push

the bag through the pocket. Press along the edge. Machine a second seam, which will enclose all raw edges. The raw edges of the pocket can be covered with bias binding which is hand sewn in place for a neater appearance. The original skirt has a small piece of cotton tape sewn between the top of the pocket bag opening and the waistband for reinforcement.

SEAMS
Join the seams of the skirt by placing right sides together and pinning through the seam lines. The edges of each seam can then be overlocked and pressed open. On the original skirt the

Detail of the back of the skirt showing the placket hole pocket and centre back fastenings.

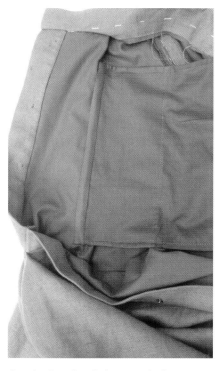

Inside skirt detail showing the bias tape sewn on top of the raw edges of the placket hole pocket.

Bottom of the centre back placket.

seams are finished by overcasting and are then pressed together to one side, away from the centre front or centre back.

CENTRE BACK PLACKET OPENING

The skirt opens at the centre back and the opening is finished with a concealed placket. The original skirt has evenly spaced hooks and eyes sewn down the placket; the reproduction skirt has snap fasteners. To make the placket, first mount the placket with Silesia and make sure the seam lines are visible on both sides. Press the seam allowance inwards along one long side. Fold the band in half lengthways with the right side facing outwards and press. Snip into the seam allowance at the bottom of the placket opening. On the right side of the skirt place the unpressed side of the placket down one side of the opening, matching the seam lines. Pin in place, stretch the opening to lie flat and pin the placket up along the other side. Machine the placket to the skirt opening, stopping at the midpoint to lift the foot of the machine and pivot the

skirt before sewing up the next side. Trim and grade the seam allowance and press along the right side of the newly sewn seam. With the raw edges of the seam enclosed, pin the free edge in place to sit just a fraction to the outside of the previous seam, and pin and tack in place. Working on the right side of the skirt, sink stitch to secure the placket in place. The placket folds into the skirt and the midpoint can be machined in a triangle to finish. Fold the placket so that when you look at the skirt the right-hand side is folded into the skirt and sits on top of the left-hand side.

THE WAISTBAND

The waistband is mounted with Silesia and is stiffened with a band of Petersham. With right sides facing, place one long side of the waistband around the edge of the waist, and pin in place through the seam lines. Tack in place and test the fit of the waistband on the wearer; adjust if necessary and then machine the waistband to the skirt along the seam line. Trim and grade the seam and push the waistband

downwards and out of the way. Working from the inside of the skirt, pin the bottom of the Petersham to the seam, just above the line of stitching and machine along the lower edge of the Petersham. Bring the waistband up behind the Petersham and fold it over so that the right sides are facing. Pin down the short ends of the waistband and machine in place. Snip off the corners and turn the right way round and fold the waistband into place. With the long raw edge turned under, pin the waistband to the skirt. Either slipstitch the waistband to the skirt, or working from the right side of the skirt, sink stitch the waistband in place (this process is also called 'stitch in the ditch'). Once the waistband has been completed, cotton tape hanging loops measuring 7.5cm on the double are attached to the original skirt using a cross stitch made with strong thread. Longer loops may be required for storage in a theatre wardrobe. Two skirt hooks and bars are sewn to the edge of the waistband to finish, using a double thread and buttonhole stitch.

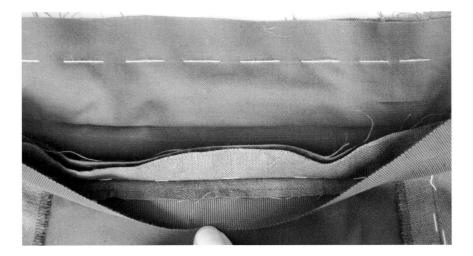

Inside view of the waistband showing the Petersham machined to the skirt seam allowance.

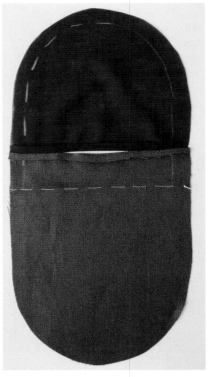

Add lining to the patch pocket.

THE WAISTBAND POCKET

This tiny pocket is made from a single rectangle of the skirt fabric measuring 12cm x 6cm plus seam allowance. It is folded in half widthways, seamed and turned through. The pocket is then sewn by hand to one side of the centre front inside the waistband. A small pocket watch or locket can be placed inside for safekeeping.

PATCH POCKET

To make the patch pocket, with right sides facing join the pocket lining to the pocket along the straight edge leaving a gap of 6cm for turning through. Press the seam and press lightly along the fold at the top edge of the pocket. With right sides facing, pin around the edge and machine along

the seam line. Trim the seam allowance and snip off the top corners and clip around the curved edge at 1cm intervals. Turn the pocket the right way round by pulling through the opening. Use a bamboo point turner to push the corners out and to make sure the edge is crisp. Press lightly and then close the gap by slipstitching by hand. The pocket is loosely gathered 3.5cm down from the top with a row of a running stitch made by hand. Thread a needle with a double thread matching the colour of the fabric and sew a row of even running stitches. Pull to lightly gather and back stitch at the other end. Make four small tucks at the bottom of the pocket, 1cm apart, from the centre front. Secure at the back by backstitching. The patch pocket is

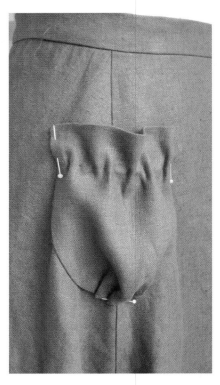

Position the patch pocket on the outside of the skirt.

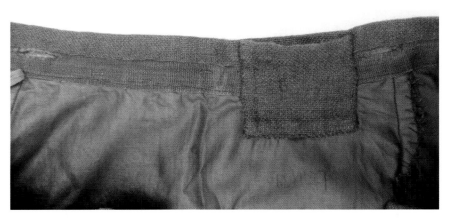

Detail of the inside of the original skirt showing the small watch pocket.

attached to the skirt by hand. Place the skirt on a dress stand if possible and position the pocket 6.5cm below the bottom of the waistband and centre it over the right side front seam. Pin in place, and the pocket can then be slipstitched around the edge. For a more secure pocket, pin the pocket in position leaving the area around the edge of the pocket free. Lift up the edge and use double thread pulled through beeswax to slipstitch the pocket to the skirt using small stitches 1cm in from the edge. To finish, use a single thread to slipstitch the pocket around the edge.

THE HEM

Skirts observed in museum collections for this book are all constructed to have hem facings. The facing used on this skirt is a separate, shaped piece of fabric 10cm deep, which is sewn to the inside of the skirt hem. The reason for a separate facing could have been that it would be easier to replace a facing rather than a whole lining if the hem became damaged from trailing along the ground. Brush braid or plain wool braid was an additional feature observed in some skirts. Brush braid was a mohair brush edge sewn around the inside hem of the skirt and it must have been especially useful for skirts with a train. The skirt pattern is marked 10cm up from the hem to give the patterns for the facings. Each facing is cut separately from mounting fabric and then joined at the side seams. The seams should be pressed open and the seam allowance along the top edge of the facings pressed under and snipped at intervals to the seam line. To join the facing to the skirt, place the facing over the bottom edge of the skirt with right sides together. Line up all seams, pin along the bottom edge and machine along the seam line. Trim the seam by grading the seam allowance. This eliminates bulk and helps it to sit better. Understitch the lining to the seam allowance and press the hem upwards, on the inside of the skirt. Pin in place and slipstitch, or herringbone if preferred. The original skirt is overcast using large stitches.

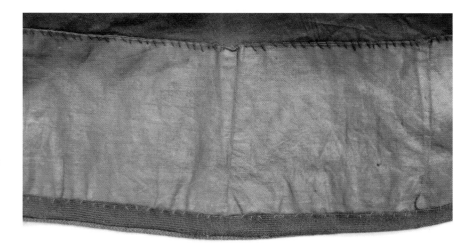

Detail of the original hem showing the facing with wool braid sewn along the bottom edge. (Worthing Museum and Art Gallery)

BODICE

Cutting and mounting

Press the fabric and if using wool shrink by hovering the steam iron close to the surface to shrink; then allow to dry. Fold the fabric in half lengthways with the selvedges matching and place all pattern pieces on the fabric with the grain lines following the straight grain of the fabric. Pin in place and add seam allowance. Pattern markings need to be transferred onto the wrong side of the centre back panels and the wrong side of the centre front panels so that the pleats and tucks can be sewn in place before mounting.

Before mounting the bodice with the striped lining, the tucks at the centre back need to be formed. There are three tucks at either side: each one is 0.5cm deep and they are machined in place and pressed away from the centre back. The original garment has a line of machining at waist level over the tucks, as indicated on the pattern. This is an additional process to help keep the tucks lying flat and facing in the same direction. The process was not done on the reproduction bodice.

The front panels have three pleats at either side of the centre front opening. The pleats are machined from the lower edge to the waist on the reverse side of the bodice and then working from the

right side the pleats pressed towards the centre front and tacked in place to make mounting easier. A dart on each side of the bodice is also closed before mounting. To close the darts, working on the wrong side of the fabric, fold the dart down the centre, pin in place and machine from the wide end to the point and press towards the centre front. At this stage close the corresponding dart in the front bodice mounting fabric.

To mount the bodice sections place the right side of each outer section face down on a flat surface and place the corresponding mounting pieces on top. When all pieces are flat and smooth, pin in place following the seam lines marked on the mounting pieces using a single thread to sew a row of tacking along each line. Mark balance points such as the shoulder point at the tip of the sleeve head and the sleeve front and back balance points.

Making order

Begin with the centre back seam. Place right sides together, pin through the seam lines, machine and press the seam open. The back side panels have curved seams; with right sides facing, pin together along the seam line starting from the lower edge with the smaller of the two pieces facing towards you. Press your thumbs into the seam and curve it in an arc to help the

Mount the centre back panels once the tucks have been machined in place.

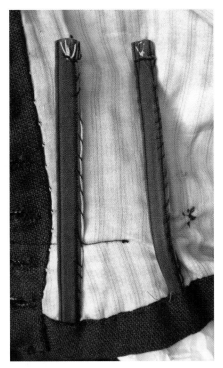

Detail of the inside of the original bodice showing the button band and the position of the boning channels with yellow flossing stitches at the tips.

seams fit together. Place the pins across the seam as well as in the seam and place under the machine foot with the shorter section on top. Machine slowly and lift the foot and pivot the needle when necessary to get a smooth curve to the seams. Press the side back seams together, away from the centre back. The next stage is to join the shoulder and side seams together by placing right sides together, pinning and machining along the seam lines and pressing the shoulder seam open and the side seams towards the centre back. The seams on the original jacket have been trimmed down to 1cm and overcast separately; on the reproduction the seams are trimmed to 1.5cm and overlocked together. If a heavier wool fabric is used for the bodice then it would be advisable to overlock the seams separately.

The original bodice is boned around the waist. Two boning channels 16cm high are sewn to the front of the mounted section before mounting takes place, and the boning is inserted into the channels once the bodice has been made up and before the hem facing is sewn in place. A further boning channel of the same length sits over the

seam at the centre back and is machined to the seam allowances. The other seams may have been boned when the bodice was made.

Finish the bottom edge of the bodice with a strip of fabric 2cm deep plus seam allowance and 75cm long. Pin the band to the outside of the bodice and machine along the seam line. Trim and grade the seams and press the band over to sit on top of the lining. Fold the top raw edge under and slipstitch to the lining.

The bodice is closed at the centre front with shank buttons and buttonholes. The button bands can either be mounted with Silesia to replicate the original bodice or a layer of fusible interfacing can be applied to the reverse side for extra strength. Fold each button band in half lengthways with right sides facing and seam across the short edges. Snip the corners, turn the right way round and press. With right sides facing and raw edges aligned, position a band along the

centre front edge. Pin and machine along the seam line. Trim and grade the seam and push all raw edges into the band. Fold the remaining raw edge under and either slipstitch in place from behind or sink stitch by machining on the right side of the bodice. Position the buttonholes down the right-hand section and ensure that when the buttons are closed they will sit in the middle of the band. The first buttonhole sits 1cm down from the upper edge and the other buttonholes are spaced 2.5cm apart. Follow instructions on your machine for sewing buttonholes. Alternatively buttonholes can be sewn by hand using buttonhole twist to match the original bodice.

MAKING THE SLEEVES

Begin by making the false cuffs, which are not lined or mounted. The pleats radiate outwards from the centre of the top and bottom seam lines. Pin the pleats in place following the directional arrows shown on the pattern and machine within the seam allowance. With right sides facing, join the seams down to the top of the opening by placing right sides together, pinning through the seam lines and machining

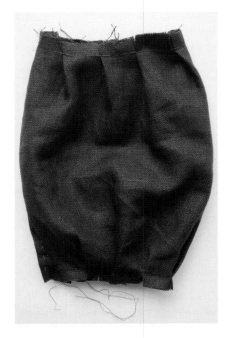

Make the false cuffs into cylinders.

and pressing the seam open. Overlock the edges of the seams and fold the cuff opening back twice and machine to a point above the opening. The lower edge is finished with a band that runs around the wrist. To make the cuff bands first mount each piece with Silesia. Fold each cuff band in half lengthways with right sides facing and seam across the short edges. Snip the corners, turn the right way round and press. With right sides facing and raw edges aligned position a band along the edge of the pleated cuff. Pin and machine along the seam line. Trim and grade the seam and push all raw edges into the band. Fold the remaining raw edge under and either slipstitch in place from behind or sink stitch by machining on the right side of the cuff. Machine one buttonhole running horizontally and a corresponding button.

The next stage is to make up the lower sleeve lining. The facing running around the edge of the lining is a separate piece, which has been marked on the bottom of the pattern piece. Alternatively, wide bias binding can be used. Bias binding can be shaped to fit a curved area by stretching and manipulating it into shape with the iron. Thread mark the seam lines on the facing, snip into the curves at 1.5cm

intervals and press the top seam allowance under. Place the facing on top of the sleeve lining, pin in place and topstitch along the fold.

With right sides facing, join the seams of the lower sleeve lining and press open. There is no need to finish the edges of the seams because they will be concealed in the jacket when it is made up. With right sides facing, slip the lining over the false cuff making sure the seams are sitting on top of each other. Tack both sections together along the upper seam line. Join the upper lining seams together by placing right sides together, machining in the seam lines and pressing open. With right sides facing slip the upper sleeve over the lower cuff, lining up the seams and with raw edges also lined up. Pin through all seam lines and tack in place. Machine around the seam lines and trim and grade the seams. Press the seams upwards towards the sleeve head.

The next stage is to join the outer sleeve to this section around the lower

edge. With right sides facing, pin all around the lower edge and then machine within the seam line. Trim the seam and snip at intervals. Turn the right way and press along the edge for a crisp finish.

Next, the lining and sleeve need to be mounted together at the sleeve head and the seam lines and balance points tacked through. Two box pleats are folded into place at the sleeve head by following the directional arrows on the pattern. Machine the pleats in place within the seam allowance.

SETTING IN THE SLEEVES

To join the sleeves to the bodice, work from the inside of the sleeve and match the balance points around the sleeve and the bodice, smoothing the sleeve into the bodice as you go. Working from the inside of the sleeve, pin vertically and horizontally and tack. Check the position of the sleeves by placing the bodice on a dress stand before machining within the seam line. Trim and overlock seams together. On

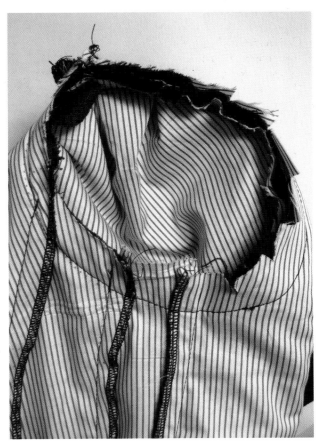

Insert the sleeves.

Add the facing along the bottom edge of
the lower sleeve lining.

the original bodice the seams are overcast separately and pressed into the sleeve.

THE COLLAR

Cut a piece of collar canvas larger than the pattern piece and trace around the edge with tailor's chalk. Place on the reverse side of the under collar, and with both sections lying on a flat surface, pin in place and tack through all layers. Machine the collar canvas along the seam line. Using a small, sharp pair of scissors, trim the seam allowance of collar canvas away, cutting close to the row of stitching. With right sides facing, pin the top collar and under collar sections together. Machine the sections together along the seam line; when passing around the corners use a small stitch and lift the machine foot and pivot to turn the collar. (Some costume makers prefer to sew one diagonal stitch across the point of the collar instead of going into the point.) Trim and grade the seams, snip the corners off, and place a drop of Fray Check at each corner for extra strength. Turn the right way round and push the corners out with the bamboo point turner or similar. Press the collar from the inside and understitch the under collar to the seam along the top as far as possible. Tack around the collar to keep in place. To

Apply a drop of Fray Check to the corners of the collar.

Prepare the collar to be attached to the bodice.

attach the collar to the bodice, with right sides facing and raw edges aligned, pin the neck edge of the outer collar to the neck edge of the bodice, matching the centre back marks. Pin and machine along the seam line. Trim and grade the seam and snip at intervals. Press the seam into the collar and fold the raw edge of the inner collar under and pin and slipstitch to the bodice. Sew two hooks and bars inside the collar using a double thread and a buttonhole stitch. The collar sits edge to edge when finished.

Finishing

To finish the collar, gather two pieces of lace together, 35cm x 3cm when gathered, and sew a piece of binding along the bottom. Slipstitch around the top of the inside of the collar so that 1cm of lace is visible.

ADAPTING THE WALKING DRESS

The skirt can easily be adapted by the addition of trimmings around the hem, and can be used with a variety of bodices or blouses. This style of skirt was popular until around 1908 when straighter skirts began to appear. The bodice could also be trimmed to make a more elaborate garment. For a quick change in the theatre, the buttons could be sewn on the opposite facing and Velcro sewn underneath.

Detail of the original bodice showing the position of the hooks at the centre front and the lace sewn to the inside of the collar. (Worthing Museum and Art Gallery)

Chapter 8
Day Dress

'To create a beautiful gown is indeed as much a work of art as to paint a beautiful picture' – so claimed the Woman's Institute of Domestic Arts & Sciences Essential Stitches and Seams booklet. The day dress featured in this chapter is from the Katherine Farebrother collection, a sub-collection at Royal Pavilion & Museums, Brighton & Hove, museum accession number C003144. It is a lightweight dress, which would have been ideal for summer days. The dress is comprised of a separate skirt and bodice made from black and cream striped cotton fabric with a jacquard woven raised pattern. The softly pleated bodice is lined but is not boned and pouches over the waistband at the sides. It has a front bib with horizontal tucks made from cream cotton lawn, lined with muslin. Like many Edwardian gowns, the back mirrors the front with details being slightly narrower at the back. Strappings of bias fabric with a row of lace braid decorate the bodice and sleeves. The sleeves are made in two parts: the lower sleeves have rows of narrow tucks and a small opening at the wrist; the upper sleeve is gathered giving the effect of a leg of mutton style. There is a simple inner bodice, which acts as a camisole; it fastens at the centre front with hooks and thread bars. The collar is made from two rows of delicate lace with a floral pattern. The collar is 7cm high in total and is supported by five composite card collar supports, each 5cm high and tacked to the inside of the collar. The bodice has four horizontal hand-worked loops evenly spaced around the waist that correspond with four hooks sewn to the inside of the waistband to help keep the bodice and skirt in place. The skirt is made from six gored panels with a centre back opening. The waistband dips at the centre front and has three bias cut pleats mounted onto a shaped waistband.

There is a small pouched bag hanging from the waistband on the right side. Strappings of bias fabric decorate the hem and are finished off with covered buttons. The dress has many fine features but it is not of the highest quality of making; there is no label and so it is possibly the work of one of the local dressmakers Katherine Farebrother was known to employ. A black tie with dangling bobbles finishes the outfit. Instructions are provided in this chapter for making the tie, but it is most likely that it was purchased separately from a vendor of novelties in ladies' neckwear.

Enlarge the pattern, add seam allowance and use it to cut and make a toile to test the shape and fit of the day dress before cutting in fabric.

Cutting

For the skirt: press the fabric and lay a single layer of fabric on a large flat surface. Begin with the skirt and the centre back panels. Each panel needs to be cut separately in order to match the centre back stripes and to ensure that they form a chevron when machined together. The centre front

Front and back illustration of the original day dress from Royal Pavilion & Museums, Brighton & Hove.

Left: The reproduction day dress.

MATERIALS AND EQUIPMENT

5 metres cotton stripe (cotton shirting
has been used for the reproduction
  dress)
2 metres cotton muslin
1 metre cotton lawn or similar
1 metre x 3cm lace for the collar
1 metre edging lace to be gathered on
  to the top edge of the collar
3 metres x 1.5cm wide straight lace
  braid
20cm black satin for the tie
2 x 2cm pompoms
Thread
Narrow plastic boning for the collar
50cm satin bias binding
Small hooks and bars
25cm medium weight fusible
  interfacing
Sewing machine

panel can be cut so that the centre front line sits on top of a vertical stripe. The side back and side front panels will not match due to the direction of the grain lines on the pattern pieces. The straight side of each panel should be placed on a wider stripe. Once pattern pieces are pinned in place add seam allowance before cutting. Tailor's tacks can be used to mark the centre back opening and the other balance marks. The horizontal pleats on the waistband are made from three bias strips with each strip measuring 7cm x 75cm. Cut three strips of white muslin to the same size to be used for mounting. Cut one piece of fusible interfacing using the waistband pattern. The decorative bands around the hem are cut on the bias and measure 5cm when cut and

2.5cm when finished; they also require muslin backing, which is also cut on the bias. To match the original skirt all stripes must be cut to follow the same direction. A further two rectangles are needed to hang the bag from the waist; these measure 1.5cm to the fold and are 28cm long when completed.

For the bodice: cut two straight sections of cream cotton fabric measuring 110cm x 30cm for the bib panels at the centre front and back. The bodice has two further front and two back panels and a peplum at the lower back. The tucks on the front of the bodice can be adjusted to follow the stripes of the fabric. The pleats and tucks on the front bodice should be marked with either tailor's tacks or an air erasable marker. The peplum is a

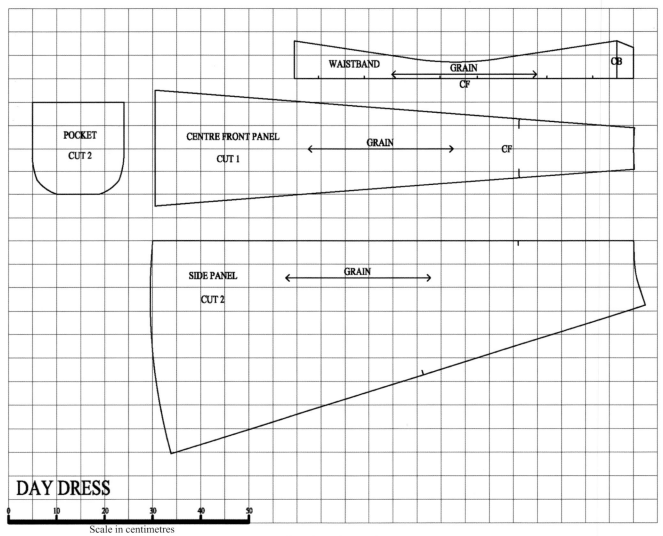

DAY DRESS

Scale in centimetres

Day dress Pattern A.

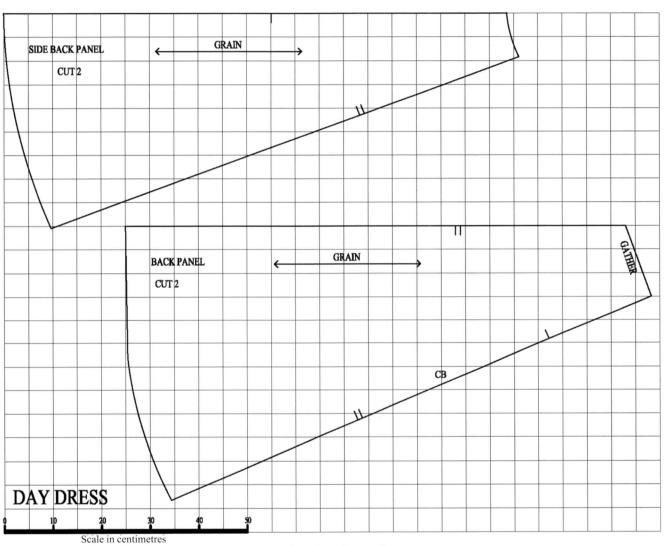

SIDE BACK PANEL

CUT 2

GRAIN

BACK PANEL

CUT 2

GRAIN

GATHER

CB

DAY DRESS

0   10   20   30   40   50

Scale in centimetres

Day dress Pattern B.

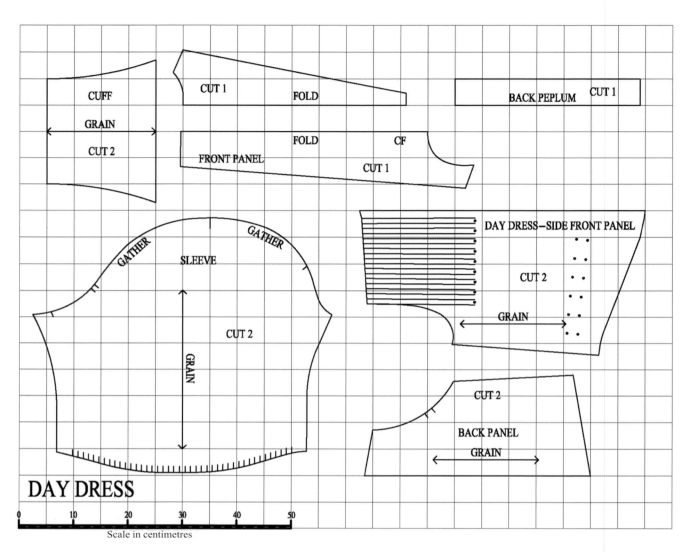

CUFF
GRAIN
CUT 2

CUT 1   FOLD

BACK PEPLUM   CUT 1

FOLD   CF

FRONT PANEL

CUT 1

DAY DRESS—SIDE FRONT PANEL

CUT 2

GRAIN

GATHER   GATHER

SLEEVE

GATHER

CUT 2

GRAIN

CUT 2

BACK PANEL

GRAIN

DAY DRESS

0   10   20   30   40   50

Scale in centimetres

Day dress Pattern C.

single piece of fabric cut on the bias. The sleeves are comprised of an upper and a lower sleeve. Cut a piece of fabric measuring 32cm x 32cm to make the tucked lower sleeve sections. Add a 3cm facing allowance to the bottom of the sleeve; this includes 2cm for the facing and 1cm for turning under to neaten the edge. The front and back bib linings are cut from muslin. The decorative bands on the bodice are cut on the bias and measure 5cm when cut and 2.5cm when completed; they also require muslin backing, which is also cut on the bias. (The original bodice has a separate in-built camisole made from lightweight muslin, fastened with hooks and bars at the centre front; this has not been included in the reproduction.)

DECORATIVE BANDS

To make the decorative bands, also known as strappings, first mount each one with bias cut muslin and press the outer seam allowances into the centre. For the bodice, only apply the mesh braid down the centre once the seam allowances have been pressed into the centre. Even though it seems more

aesthetically pleasing to have the stripes forming a chevron, the stripes on the museum's skirt and bodice all face in the same direction. Cover the buttons used as decoration on the skirt with the striped fabric following the guidelines on the packet. Sew the buttons in place with a double thread at the top of each point. The stripes on the original buttons all face downwards. Wrapping the thread tightly around the shank before backstitching helps the button to stay in place and keeps the stripe vertical.

BODICE

Making order

FRONT AND BACK SIDE BODICE
Begin by forming the tucks that fall from the shoulders in the front side bodice sections by folding along the lines indicated on the pattern. Pin, machine and press one tuck at a time before moving on to the next. When all tucks are completed press them away

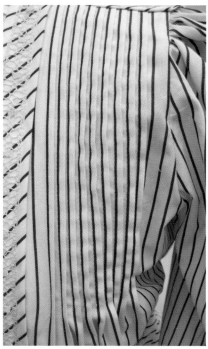

Tucks flowing down from the shoulder at the side front.

from the centre front to face the armhole. The front side bodice pieces have pleats at the waist to create the pouched effect and these are formed by pinching the pleats together on the reverse side and machining a vertical line to hold each one in place. The back panels also have pleats at the waist which can be pinned and machined in place within the seam allowance.

BIB PIECES WITH TUCKS
To make the bib tucks, measure 2cm down from the top of the cream cotton fabric making sure the line is sitting along the straight grain of the weft thread. Using an air erasable marker draw a straight line, and then draw a further line 0.5cm apart. Fold along the final line and press. Machine 0.5cm down from the fold using the marked line as a guide. Push the tuck away from the top and on the wrong side press flat. Press on the right side and measure 0.5cm from the fold and a further 0.5cm. Press along the outer line and repeat the process until the section is filled with tucks. Alternatively

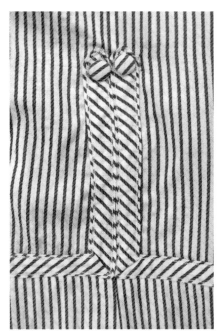

Detail of the original skirt showing the decorative strips applied around the hem with covered buttons at the tips.

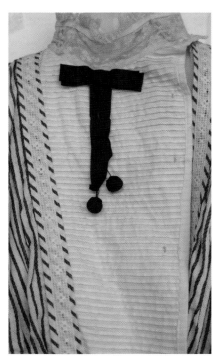

Detail of the bodice of the original day dress open at the left hand side showing the position of the hand worked loops.

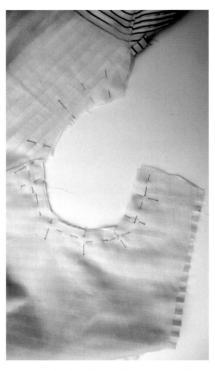

Marking the tucks for the bib using a Pattern Master and an air erasable marker.

Lay the bodice flat and pin the muslin lining around the neck.

Fold the muslin lining behind the bibs and pin to the seam allowances.

mark the whole section in stripes 2.5cm apart, each stripe being the fold line for a tuck. The tucks on the original bibs are 3mm wide with a gap of 3mm between each tuck. Cut out the front and back bib sections using the tucked panels with all tucks facing downwards. Cut out the same shapes from muslin.

JOINING THE BIB AND BODICE PANELS

The front and back bib sections are sandwiched in place before the front and back bodice sections are joined together. Begin by making up the back of the bodice. With right sides facing place the bib to the bodice and pin and machine within the seam lines. Press the seams away from the centre front. Join the right-hand side bodice section to the right side of the front bib, and with right sides facing place the bib to the bodice and pin and machine within the seam lines. Press the seam away from the centre front. Overlock the edge of the left front side bodice and press the seam allowance under along

the seam line. Join the shoulder seams by placing right sides together and pinning and machining along the seam line. Press the seam open and overlock the edges.

The neck edge of the bodice is neatened by the muslin lining. Join the shoulder seam on the right-hand side of the muslin lining using a narrow French seam or an open seam. Lay the bodice on a flat surface with the right side facing upwards. With right sides facing, place the muslin lining on top of the bib section. Pin together around the neck and shoulders along the seam lines. Leave the left-hand side of the front bib open. Machine along the seam line and trim to 0.5cm and snip into the curved edge around the neck at 1cm intervals. Turn the right way round and press before topstitching 0.5cm in from the neckline. Fold the muslin lining to the inside of the bodice and line up all raw edges. Pin and tack in place and overlock the edges; the lining will finally be held in place by the two rows of machining used to attach the decorative strips,

which will be added once the sleeves are in place.

The open edge of the bib is finished with a binding made from cream cotton. Cut a bias strip 4cm wide and 56cm long. Fold the long edges into the centre and press. Working from the back of the bib place one edge of the binding along the raw edge and pin and machine down the pressed line. Fold the binding round to the front of the bib, tuck the top end in and pin through all layers of the binding and machine close to the folded edge. A row of thread bars is worked in blanket stitch down the seam line of the left side of the bib, 3cm apart. A row of corresponding hooks is sewn under the strapping on the left-hand side of the bodice when the bodice is completed.

SLEEVES

To make the tucks, measure 6cm down from the top edge of the fabric piece and draw the first line with an air erasable marker. Fold along the line and press. Machine 0.5cm away from the fold to form the first tuck. Press the

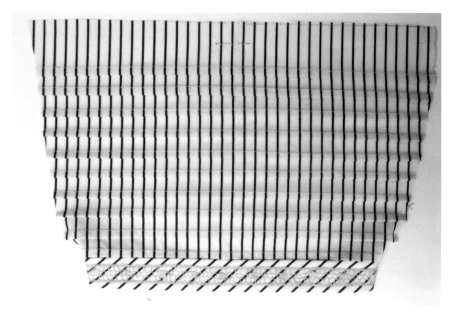

Sew tucks in the lower sleeve.

Gather the top sleeve to fit the lower sleeve and add the decorative bands.

tuck downwards. Measure 1.5cm from the folded edge and press along the fold line. Machine 0.5cm down from the fold to form the second tuck and machine in place. Repeat until 10 tucks are sewn. Place a decorative strip along the bottom of the fabric with the edge of the tuck butting up against the edge of the strip; pin and machine in place along the edge of the braid. Press the facing over by 1cm and machine along the edge.

Position the pattern piece on top of the lower sleeve and mark around the edge, add seam allowance and cut out. Fold the facing round to the front, stitch down the sides within the seam allowance and snip off the corners. Turn the facing the right way round so that it sits at the back of the sleeve. Slipstitch the facing to the sleeve. On the original bodice the fullness in the upper sleeve at the sleeve head and at the elbow is reduced with tucks that are unevenly spaced. The reproduction sleeve pattern is gathered at the sleeve head and has tucks at the elbow. To make the gathers, set the machine to the longest stitch and sew two parallel lines behind the seam line and within the seam allowance, approximately 0.3cm and 0.6cm apart. Knot the four threads at one end and pull to gather using the top threads at the other end. Check that the measurement fits between the notches marked around the armhole on the bodice and knot the threads at the other end. Distribute the gathers evenly and, using only the tip of the iron, press along the gathers, within the seam allowance. To join to the upper and lower sleeve place right sides together and pin along the seam line; pin and machine together. Trim the seam allowance down to 1cm and overlock the edges together. Lightly press the seam allowance upwards. Place the sleeve on a flat surface facing upwards and pin the decorative band in place along the top of the lower sleeve and just covering the upper sleeve; machine along the edges of the braid to secure.

To join the sleeve seams place right sides together and pin along the seam line. Use pins to match up the

With right sides facing pin the sleeve along the seam line.

pressed under to neaten the edge. The underside is finished off by slipstitching the seam. Centre the lace braid on top of the epaulettes leaving an extra 1cm to overhang at the point. Machine in place down both edges and finish off by folding the braid over the pointed edge and slipstitching in

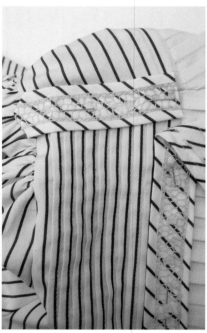

Centre the epaulettes over the shoulder seam.

decorative bands and tucks. Machine, and overlock the seam allowances and press together to one side. Sew a hook and bar at the wrist so that the cuff overlaps slightly.

SETTING IN THE SLEEVES

To join the sleeves to the bodice, work from the inside of the sleeve and match the balance points around the sleeve and the bodice, smoothing the sleeve into the bodice as you go. Pin vertically and horizontally and machine within the seam line, working from the inside of the sleeve. Trim and overlock the edges together. On the original bodice the upper sleeve has a separate and narrower lining joined from the top of the lower sleeve to the armhole and the armhole is encased with a binding to finish all raw edges. The pattern piece can be used to make the lining by folding some of the fullness away.

EPAULETTES AND DECORATIVE STRIPS

The epaulettes are cut on the cross grain of the fabric and on the original garment the stripes face the same direction on both epaulettes. To make, place the pattern on the right side of the fabric, place carbon paper underneath and use a tracing wheel to trace around the edge. Tack along this line to thread mark the outline of the epaulette. The epaulettes on the original garment do not feel as if they

contain any interlining. Because the fabric I am using is slightly lighter than the original, I tacked a layer of muslin behind the epaulette to use as an interlining. Beginning with the points, press the seam allowance inwards, then press in the sides. I added an extra 0.5cm to one of the sides and this was

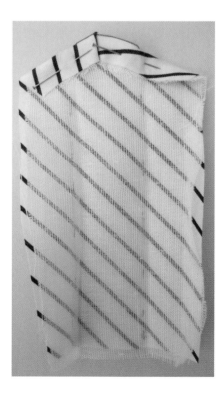

Mount the epaulette with muslin and fold into shape with a pointed end.

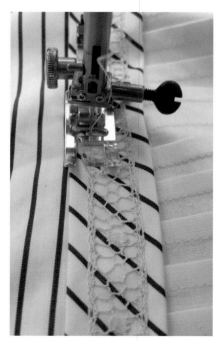

Machine the decorative band to the bodice.

place from behind.

To add the epaulettes to the bodice, centre them over the shoulder seam with the pointed end of the epaulette sitting over the sleeve head by 1cm. Pin and machine in place by sewing along the edges of the lace braid. Place the bodice on a dress stand if possible and centre the decorative strips to sit along the side bodice seam line. At the left front edge the strip will overhang the seam line which has already been folded behind. Machine the strips to the bodice by sewing along the edges of the lace braid.

PEPLUM AND BODICE HEM

Finish the back of the bodice by adding the peplum. To make the peplum, neaten the two short edges and the lower edge by folding the seam allowance over twice and machining. Fold the pleats into the top of the peplum and machine within the seam allowance. Match the centre of the peplum to the centre back mark at the end of the bib and with right sides facing pin the peplum to the bodice. Machine in place along the seam line and overlock all edges together and press the seam downwards. Finish the front hem of the bodice by folding the seam allowance over twice and machining.

LACE COLLAR

The finished collar on the reproduction garment measures 39cm although this measurement can be adjusted to suit the preference of the wearer. The widest part of the collar is made from two straight pieces of lace with a repeating pattern. The pattern is mirrored on the top and bottom layer of the collar, so to join the pieces together, begin by laying one on top of the other, matching up the pattern. Pin in place and line up the edges. Using a short, wide zigzag stitch, sew along the edges to join together. Open out and press flat. The collar is trimmed at the upper edge with gathered lace, which may have originally been bought as a readymade piece because it is gathered onto a piece of linen that is not used elsewhere in the dress. To make a gathered section of lace, use the longest machine stitch to sew two rows along the bottom edge. Tie a knot in all threads at one side and then pull the top two threads at the other end to gather. Check the measurement against the straight section and knot at the other end. Press the lace lightly using the tip of the iron, staying within the seam allowance. Pin the gathers behind the top of the collar and machine in place. To neaten the front of the collar make a bias strip 2cm wide and 42cm long. Press the long edges into the centre. Place the strip on the right side of the collar and centre it over the join between the top of the collar and the frill. Pin and machine, sewing close to the outside edges. The raw edges behind the collar are enclosed by hand

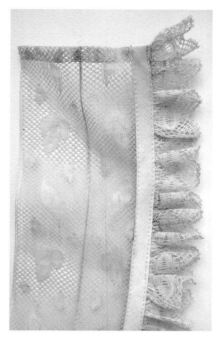

Make the lace collar.

sewing a strip of narrow bias binding on top but leaving the bottom edge open for inserting the collar supports. This edge is hand sewn to the collar supports once they are in position.

The original blouse has five 5cm high composite card collar supports attached at regular intervals around the collar. The supports are loosely hand sewn to the lace collar in order to make removal easy when the collar needed to be washed. Although it is no longer possible to buy composite collar supports, substitutes can be made by covering plastic boning with readymade satin bias binding.

The collar is fastened at the centre back with three thread bars and metal hooks. Fold the short end of the right-hand side of the collar under by 0.5cm and then a further 0.5cm and slipstitch. Thread bars are sewn on top of this seam. To make a thread bar, thread a needle with a double thread and make a knot in the end. Start with a back stitch and make a loop wide enough for the hook and backstitch. Bring the thread to the surface and work a tight blanket stitch along the loop until you reach the other end. Finish with a final backstitch. The three corresponding hooks on the other side of the collar

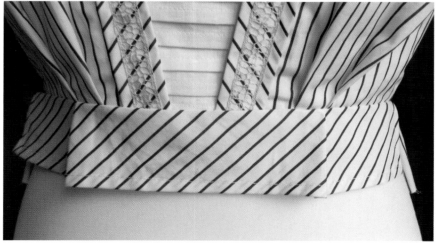

Add the peplum to the lower back bodice.

(which is also folded twice and slipstitched) can also be sewn on with a blanket stitch. The collar is attached to the bodice once the bodice has been completed.

NECK TIE

The original neck tie is 8cm wide across the top of the bow and 13cm long from the top of the bow to the bottom of the lower tie. Cut four strips of black satin measuring 6cm x 18cm. With right sides facing, fold in half lengthways and machine down the long edge. Turn two of the strips the right way round and press. Construct the tie by forming a double bow with a section wrapped around the middle. Sew a V shape at the ends of the other two strips with the seam in the centre. Trim around the point and dab a drop of Fray Check before turning through and pressing. These two pieces are used for the dangling sections of the tie and one is 2.5cm longer than the other when they are layered together. A

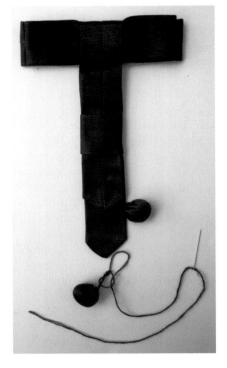

Use embroidery thread to make a chain loop from the lower points of the tie to the top of the bobbles.

Assemble the neck tie.

section of the strip is wrapped firmly around the ties 2cm down from the bottom edge of the bow and hand sewn in place from behind.

To make the bobbles cut two circles of fabric big enough to cover the

pompoms. Sew a small running stitch around the edge of the circle, place a pompom in the centre and pull the threads to gather. Finish off by oversewing. There will be a frayed edge and so trim the most prominent threads and cover the area with Fray Check and allow to dry. To attach the bobbles to the ends of the tie use three strands of embroidery thread and make a chain measuring 2cm long, starting at the bobble and finishing with a backstitch towards the back of the ends of the tie. A small safety pin can be sewn to the back of the tie and used for attaching the tie to the front neck where the collar and bodice meet. The original tie is hand sewn to the front of the collar.

SKIRT

Making order

JOINING THE SEAMS

Begin by joining the centre front panel to the side front panels by placing right sides together and matching the balance marks and seam lines, then pin and machine. The seams can then be overlocked together and pressed away from the centre front or overlocked separately and pressed open. The seam allowance on the original skirt is 1cm. The seam edges are unfinished and are pressed together to one side. The side panels should next be joined to the back panels; the centre back seam is

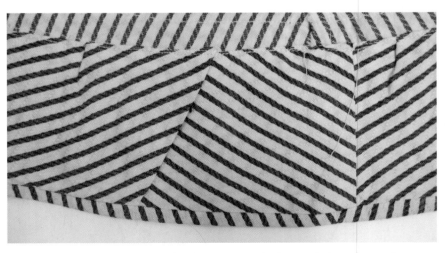

Detail showing the original skirt facing cut on the bias and pleated into place.

the last to be joined and before this the decorative strips should be applied to the skirts. Tack the strips into place and form into a point 18cm high from the tip to the bottom of the band, mitre the corners. The bottom edge of each finished strip sits 8cm up from the bottom edge of the hem. The hem facing, which is cut on the bias, is 10cm deep when finished. The hem facing can be machined to the skirt because the decorative bands will cover this when they are machined around the skirt.

CENTRE BACK PLACKET

The skirt opens at the centre back and the opening is finished with a concealed placket with horizontal stripes. The original skirt has evenly spaced hooks and eyes sewn down the placket; the reproduction skirt has snap fasteners. Mount the placket with muslin or fusible interfacing and make sure the seam lines are visible on the wrong side. Press the seam allowance inwards along one long side. Fold the band in half lengthways with the right side facing outwards and press. On the right side of the skirt place the un-pressed side of the placket down one side of the opening matching the seam lines. Pin in place, stretch the opening to lie flat and pin the placket along the other side. Cut into the seam at the bottom of the placket. Machine the placket to the skirt opening, stopping at the midpoint to lift the foot of the machine and pivot the skirt before sewing up the next side. Trim and grade the seam allowance and press along the right side of the newly sewn seam. With the raw edges of the seam enclosed, pin the free edge in place to sit just a fraction to the outside of the previous seam, and tack in place. Working on the right side of the skirt, sink stitch to secure the placket in place. The placket folds into the skirt and the midpoint can be machined in a triangle to finish. Fold the placket so that when you look at the skirt the right-hand side is folded into the skirt and sits on top of the left-hand side. Space three sets of snap fasteners equally down the centre of the placket and sew

Detail showing the original back placket with horizontal stripes.

firmly in place using a double thread and a blanket stitch.

POUCHED BAG

The bag is unlined and is constructed of two pieces joined together at the sides by a French seam that sits on the outside of the bag. To form the seam, place right sides together and machine 0.5cm away from the seam line, trim to 0.3cm, turn the bag inside out and press along the seam line. Sew a further seam 0.5cm in from the edge. Fold the facing to the inside and press along the fold line. Open up and press the raw edge over by 1.5cm. Fold the facing back inside the bag. Mark the casing with an air erasable marker 3cm down from the top of the bag and a further 1cm below this line. Pin and machine the facing to the bag along these lines to form the casing. Leave an opening at the back of the bag for threading the elastic through. Pull the elastic to gather the casing until the bag measures 14cm across at this point. Overstitch the elastic and machine the casing gap closed. To make the ties that join the bag to the waistband, fold the

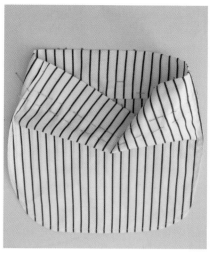

The top of the elastic casing pinned 3cm down from the top of the bag.

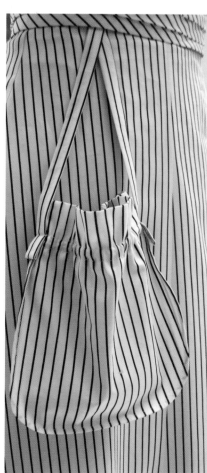

The finished pouched bag hanging from the waistband.

fabric in half lengthways and machine down the side and across one end. Trim and turn the right way round and press. Fold the finished end over by 2.5cm and centre each tie over the side seam and machine in place along the top of the casing.

WAISTBAND

The waistband is shaped to dip at the centre front and gradually rise to a peak at the centre back. It has three rows of folded bias cut strips applied to the front of the waistband, which follow the shape of the waistband. To prepare the bias strips mount each one onto a strip of muslin using long diagonal tacking stitches. Press two of the strips in half with the right side facing outwards. The other strip should be pressed under by 1cm along one long edge only – this is the middle strip. Take the front waistband piece and apply fusible interfacing to the reverse, making sure all seam lines are visible on both sides of this piece. To assemble the waistband, begin by positioning the bottom folded bias strip. This hangs 1cm below the seam line and when the skirt is assembled this section hides the skirt and waistband seam. Pin and tack in place, taking care to keep the bias strip lying flat. Measure up 1.5cm from the folded edge at the centre front and mark a line. Take the strip that has been pressed under by 1cm and position the folded edge along the marked line at the centre front and lift at the centre back. Working from inside, machine along the fold and then press this section upwards. It should hang down slightly and the diagonal lines should match at the centre front. Pin and tack it in place along the top raw edge. Take the third section and position it 2cm up from the previous folded edge at the centre front and swing it out to run along the top of the waistband at the back. Pin and tack in place and machine.

Take the inside facing waistband piece and place on top of the front section with right sides together. Follow the tacked lines, pin in place and machine along the seam line. Grade the seam allowance to reduce bulk and snip off the corners. Place a dab of Fray Check on the corners and allow to dry before turning the right way round. Understitch along the top edge of the waistband as far as possible. Press the waistband to lie flat. Place the pattern piece on top to check the measurements. Add the centre front line and the line to mark the wrap over of the waistband at the centre back. The waistband is attached to the skirt in a back to front way. The inside of the waistband is machined in place first and the front is slipstitched afterwards. To finish, a covered piece of boning is sewn to the inside of the right centre back and three sets of hooks and bars are added.

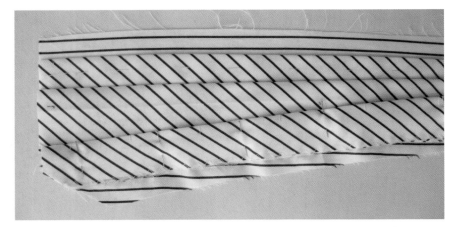

Layer the three long bias strips to the front of the waistband, lifting them at the centre back.

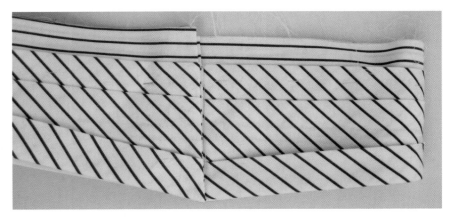

The centre back waistband.

FINISHING

The collar opens at the centre back and is hand sewn to the neck edge around the right-hand side of the bodice, starting at the centre back and then continuing around the front bib and stopping 2.5cm from the shoulder seam to allow the front bib to slide under the back when the bodice is worn. To finish the collar, sew three hooks along the bottom of the left side of the lace collar and sew three thread bars around the left back neck edge. Place the completed bodice and skirt on a dress stand and pin the bottom edge of the lace collar on top of the neck. The bottom edge of the collar sits 0.5cm away from the neck edge and can follow the line of topstitching. Slipstitch in place with small stitches.

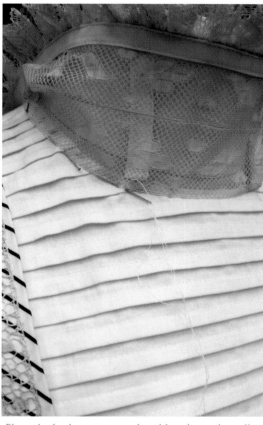

Place the bodice on a stand and hand sew the collar.

ADAPTING THE DAY DRESS

The skirt can be made up in a plain fabric without the decorative trimming. A straight waistband could be attached like the waistband used in Chapter 7. The skirt could also be made up in wool and mounted onto Silesia or a similar cotton backing. For a quick change Velcro could be used as a method of fastening on the placket of the skirt, although it is advisable to use a skirt hook and bar on the waistband. The bodice pattern could also be used to make a blouse, and the necktie could be replaced with an Edwardian brooch.

Detail showing the original collar with composite card collar supports and a row of hooks along the back edge and at the centre back.

Chapter 9
Evening Gown

In 1907 'Penelope', a fashion writer for the upmarket weekly journal The Ladies' Field, *wrote an article considering the drawbacks of unadventurous evening gowns:*

> There is generally a time in a woman's life when she absolutely sighs for a gown which is out of the common – distinguished, artistic. One gets so terribly tired of the ordinary fashionable garb, no matter how prettily it is carried out, and the sure knowledge that a hundred, more or less, exact reproductions of one's self will be present at every crowded gathering, is, after a time, somewhat depressing.

The solution to her dilemma would have been either to make her own gown or to commission an exclusive design from a dressmaker. The black satin evening gown featured in this chapter is exquisitely beaded by hand-making it unlikely that the wearer would encounter someone else in the same gown at an evening function. The gown is part of the collection at Worthing Museum, museum accession number 1970/802/2. It is listed with an approximate date of c.1918 although the high-waisted column gown also known as the Directoire waist also corresponds to designs from earlier in the decade. A sketch of a black gown c.1912 drawn by fashion illustrator Ida Pritchard has similar features.

The dress wraps over at the front and opens on the left-hand side to reveal a foundation bodice and underskirt. The outer body of the dress is in good condition, the satin is unmarked and the chiffon sleeves and detailing are intact. Like many Edwardian gowns the back of the bodice mirrors the front. The bodice has front and back inserted

panels of tulle, which are decorated with a geometric design formed from black cord braid with pearlescent sequined flower motifs and silver star-shaped sequins held in place with small gunmetal beads. Below the waist the back of the dress has a small train cut as a separate panel that falls to the left side only. At the centre front the

skirt parts to reveal a satin panel sewn to an underskirt. A black satin flower marks the spot where the skirt opens. The dress has been constructed to hang off a cream silk boned foundation bodice; the silk is fragile and has begun to disintegrate in places. Around the inside of the neck of the foundation bodice sits a casing and the original

Black Empire-style evening gown sketched by fashion illustrator Ida Pritchard. (Worthing Museum and Art Gallery)

Left: The reproduction evening gown.

narrow tape drawstrings can still be seen. The purpose of the drawstrings was to ensure a snug fit to the body of the wearer. The foundation bodice fastens with hooks and eyes at the centre front and it is secured to the body at the waist through a woven twill waist stay.

The waist stay is printed with the details E. & M. Hull, 59 Chepstow Place, Bayswater, and the single W is used in place of West London. This was the manufacturer of the foundation bodice but it may not have been the manufacturer of the evening gown. There is a small hole in the bodice that has been patched and repaired close to the centre front opening, which suggests that the bodice is older than the rest of the dress and may have been used as the foundation of a previous garment. A belt worn at the waist around the outside of the dress is made from a layer of net, heavily encrusted with black glass or jet beads. The belt is lined with satin and fastens at the side front. In 1909 *The Drapers' Record* reported the popularity of jet cabochon beads used as decoration on evening gowns. One particular example, a black net tabard, was covered with jet cabochons, which made it extremely heavy. The beads used on the Worthing museum dress appear to be a mixture of jet cabochons and glass beads. Large flat single beads are sewn to the top of each shoulder with two further beads used to form narrow horizontal pleats near the hem at the right-hand side. The long floaty sleeves are formed of panels of chiffon with beaded tassels sewn to each of the four lower points. Two further panels of chiffon are gathered onto the waist to form side

Illustration of the front and back view of the original evening gown.

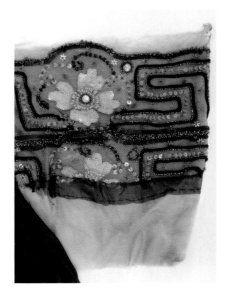

Front beaded panel of the original gown.

Inside the evening gown, showing the waist stay printed with the name and address of the original dressmakers.

Detail of the shoulder of the original
gown with a flat bead centred over the
shoulder seam.

Detail showing the back view of the original evening gown, which mirrors the front
view.

panels that lie over the skirt.
Enlarge the patterns, add seam
allowance and use them to cut and
make a toile to test the shape and fit of
the evening gown before cutting in
fabric.

Cutting

Note the direction given on the skirt
pattern pieces for placing the pattern
on the fabric. The satin skirt panels
should all be placed on the satin as
indicated on the pattern to ensure that
the train sits on the left-hand side of the
body. Both pieces of the underskirt are
cut on the fold. A rectangle of fabric
and fusible interfacing measuring 6cm
x 60cm are also needed to form the
placket on the underskirt; this includes
0.5cm seam allowance. A false front for
the underskirt is cut from satin
following the shape marked out on the
underskirt pattern. An additional hem
allowance should be added to the
bottom edge of the false underskirt
panel of 11cm; this includes a 5cm hem
and 6cm for facing the hem. The outer
bodice is cut in satin and is unlined.
The tulle bodice panels have a single
layer of black net on top. The
foundation bodice is cut from silk
habutai. All chiffon pieces should be
cut out on a folded piece of fabric
following the grain line marked on the
pattern. Add a generous seam
allowance to all pattern pieces. All
seams and balance marks should be
tacked through to the right side of the
fabric.

MATERIALS

Outer dress and scarf
4 metres black satin
4 x 5cm black beaded tassels
4 x 2cm pompoms
Stranded gold embroidery thread
3 metres chiffon

Underskirt
1.5 metres black cotton fabric
5 black snap fasteners

Foundation bodice
50cm lightweight cream silk habutai
1 metre x 22mm cotton twill tape
1.5 metres narrow cotton tape for the neck casing
Hooks and eyes/bars

Net panels and beading
50cm black net
1 metre lightweight cream tulle
5mm matt black flat sequins
5mm mother of pearl flat sequins
6mm black bugle beads
7mm black glass faceted beads
28g x 9/0 gunmetal seed beads
28g x 9/0 black seed beads
2 x 12mm mother of pearl domed buttons
8 x 2.5cm faceted beads, flat on one side, or domed buttons, oval shaped if possible
2 metres x 3mm black cord braid

EQUIPMENT
Thread
Beading needles
Embroidery hoop
Bamboo point turner
Sewing machine
Pinking shears
Dress stand

Making order
FOUNDATION BODICE

The original bodice has two layers of insertion lace hand sewn below the neck edge; this has not been included on the reproduction garment or on the pattern. There is a further trim of narrow lace around the armholes, which has also been omitted. To make the bodice, begin by inserting the gussets into the front panels: on the inside, with right sides facing, pin the gusset in place and machine. Before any further seams are machined the bodice should be fitted to the wearer to ensure a snug fit. To do this all seams should be pinned and tacked and then a fitting can take place. The original bodice has seams finished by oversewing but the reproduction can either be overlocked or the edges of the

Centre back boning channel.

seam allowance turned over and machined with a straight stitch.

To form the boning channels, pin cotton tape on top of the open seams and machine down either side and across the top. Insert plastic boning into the channels and, using a zipper foot, machine across the bottom to secure the bone in place. The boning needs to be either melted at either end or bound with cotton tape to make sure it does not poke through the boning channels. The bodice fastens with hook and eye tape that is folded in half lengthways and machined on to the facing at the front of the bodice. Make the facings into boning channels and insert further boning at the centre fronts to the side of the hook and eye tape. Secure in place at the top and bottom. To finish the raw edges around the top of the foundation bodice a facing cut on the bias is sewn along the inside. This forms a casing which a cotton tape passes through in order to gather the neckline in to fit the wearer at the centre back. To make the facing, cut two bias strips 2.5cm x 50cm. Fold the bias strips in half lengthways and press and machine down the inside of one short edge on either piece. Place the strip along the outside of the bodice with the raw edges lining up. Machine along the seam line and trim and layer the seam to eliminate as much bulk as possible. Fold the facings to the inside of the bodice and in place. Leaving the centre back open, machine along the bottom of the casing. Attach a small safety pin to the cotton tape and pass through both casings. Secure in place at the centre fronts and leave

Inside view of the reproduction foundation bodice.

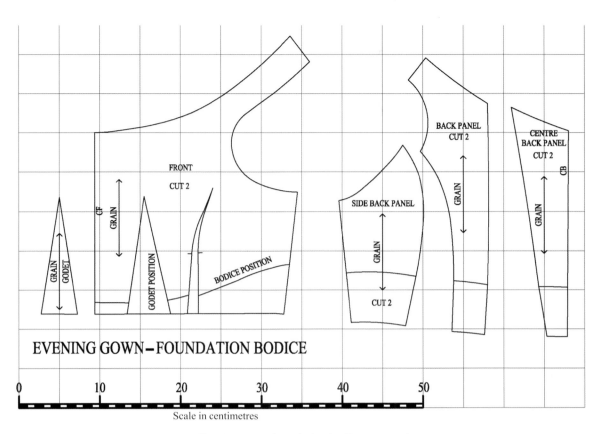

EVENING GOWN – FOUNDATION BODICE

GODET

GRAIN

CF GRAIN

FRONT
CUT 2

GODET POSITION

BODICE POSITION

SIDE BACK PANEL

GRAIN

CUT 2

BACK PANEL
CUT 2

GRAIN

CENTRE
BACK
PANEL
CUT 2

GRAIN

CB

```
0        10        20        30        40        50
```
Scale in centimetres

Evening gown foundation bodice pattern A.

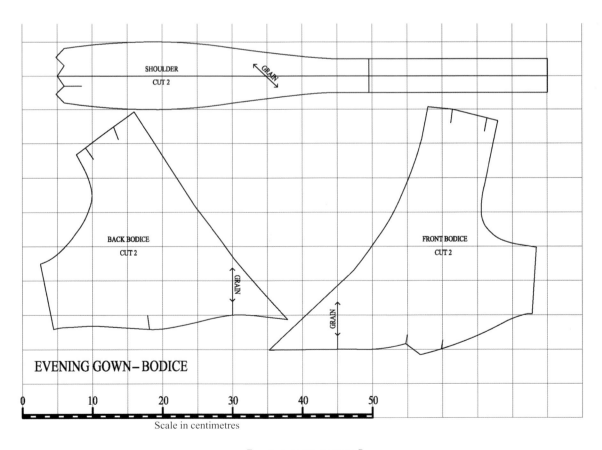

EVENING GOWN – BODICE

SHOULDER
CUT 2

GRAIN

BACK BODICE
CUT 2

GRAIN

FRONT BODICE
CUT 2

GRAIN

```
0        10        20        30        40        50
```
Scale in centimetres

Evening gown pattern B.

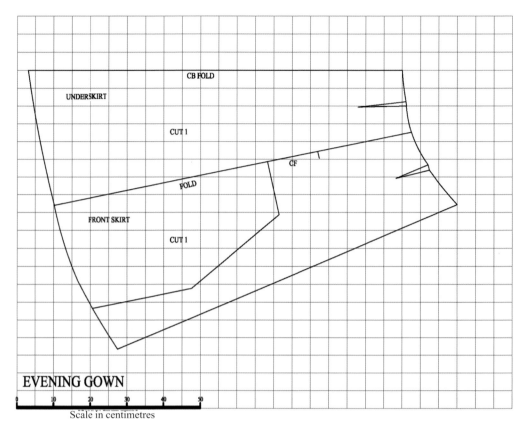

CB FOLD

UNDERSKIRT

CUT 1

CF

FOLD

FRONT SKIRT

CUT 1

EVENING GOWN

Scale in centimetres
0   10   20   30   40   50

Evening gown pattern C.

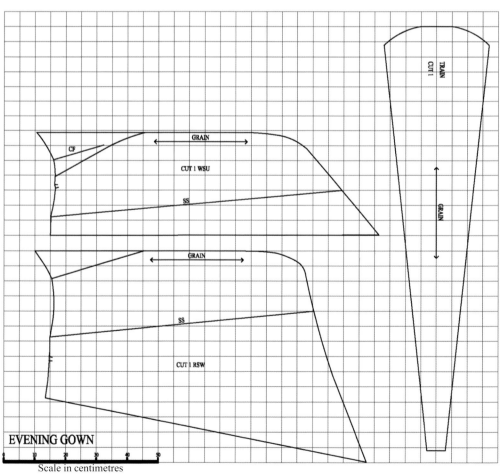

TRAIN
CUT 1

GRAIN

CF

CUT 1 WSU

GRAIN

SS

GRAIN

SS

CUT 1 RSW

EVENING GOWN

Scale in centimetres
0   10   20   30   40   50

Evening gown pattern D.

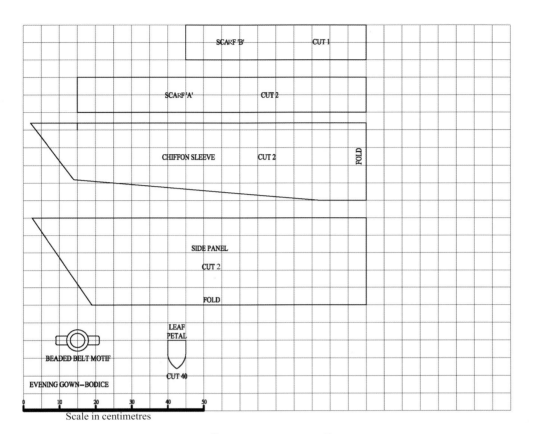

SCARF 'B'   CUT 1

SCARF 'A'   CUT 2

CHIFFON SLEEVE   CUT 2   FOLD

SIDE PANEL

CUT 2

FOLD

LEAF
PETAL

BEADED BELT MOTIF

CUT 40

EVENING GOWN—BODICE

0   10   20   30   40   50

Scale in centimetres

Evening gown pattern E.

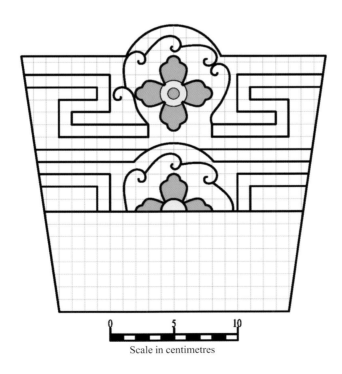

0   5   10

Scale in centimetres

Evening gown beaded panel F.

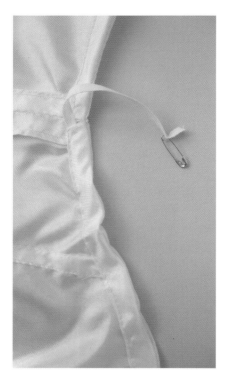

Casing around the neck edge of the foundation bodice.

Hook and eye tape is sewn at the centre front.

the long ends of the tape at the centre back. The bottom edge of the bodice is finished with bias binding.

UNDERSKIRT

The underskirt is a long A-line skirt made from a front and a back panel. The underskirt opens at the centre front with a false placket. The underskirt is made like a lining so all darts and seams are on the outside leaving the inside, which sits against the body, looking neat and tidy. Begin by closing the darts: pin and machine the darts from the wide end to the point. Dressmakers may prefer to knot the ends of the dart rather than reverse stitching; as a costume maker time is often in short supply and so careful reverse stitching exactly along the same line is preferable. Press the darts inwards to face the centre front and centre back.

To make the placket, first apply the fusible interfacing to the reverse side and make sure all seam lines are still

Placket detail, centre front underskirt.

visible. The placket is then placed against the inside of the skirt, and taking a 0.5cm seam allowance from the newly cut opening, pin the placket in place with right sides facing and raw edges aligned. Machine down one edge until reaching the midpoint, lift the foot and pivot the skirt to get across the corner, machine up the other side, and press the seam allowance into the placket. Fold the placket along the fold line and turn the seam allowance under. Pin the placket in place and topstitch close to the edge.

The foundation bodice with sleeves sewn around the armholes and the underskirt sewn on top.

The next process is to join the side seams: with right sides facing pin and machine along the seam lines. The seams on the original skirt are left unfinished but on the reproduction skirt they can be overlocked together before pressing towards the back. Press the hem upwards, fold twice to neaten the edge and topstitch in place.

The underskirt has a false front made from satin that sits below the placket and is shaped at the sides. To make the false front begin by hemming it, press over 1cm along the bottom raw edge and machine in place. With right sides facing press the hem upwards and pin down the sides. Machine the sides of the hem, snip off the corners, trim the seam and turn through. Press the hem lightly along the folded edge only and slipstitch the hem to the fabric taking care that the stitches do not show through to the front. Press the remaining seam allowances under and position the false front on top of the underskirt. It is useful to insert something to prevent pins from going through both layers, a Pattern Master is ideal. Pin the false front in place and then topstitch to the front layer by machining around the folded edge.

The underskirt is attached to the foundation bodice around the waist and sits on the outside of the foundation bodice. Prepare the underskirt for attachment by turning the seam allowance over inwards along the top edge and machining; this edge will be completely enclosed when the gown is finished. Place the bodice on the stand and pin the underskirt in place following the line indicated on the pattern. On the original bodice the underskirt is attached with tacking stitches by hand but it can be machined in place on the reproduction garment.

OUTER BODICE

The satin outer bodice wraps over at the front and back. The front bodice dips at the centre front and the fullness is reduced at the bottom edge with tucks and gathering. Begin by joining the shoulder seams: pin right sides together and machine along the seam

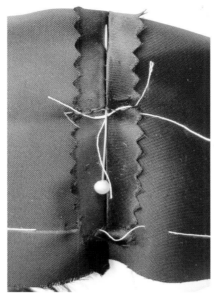

Pleat sewn on the reverse side of the shoulder.

line. Press the seam open; the edges of the original bodice are left raw but on the reproduction they are cut with pinking shears. The seams could be overlocked but there is a risk that the overlocking will leave an imprint on the right side of the satin when the seams are pressed. The shoulder seams have a pleat and this can be folded and machined in place on the reverse side.

Before joining the side seams, finish the armholes by cutting two 4cm x 50cm bias strips. Fold each strip in half lengthways with the right sides facing outwards and press. Use tailor's chalk to draw a 0.5cm seam allowance in from the raw edge. Pin on the outside of the armhole with the raw edges facing the armhole. Machine in place and trim the armhole seams down to 0.5cm. Press the binding over the seams and to the inside of the armhole. Pin and tack in place and then machine in the ditch created by the seam.

The side seams can be joined by the same method as the shoulder seams. Large flat beads or buttons can be sewn on top of the shoulders at this stage. The neck edges of the bodice are finished with a fold of chiffon at either side. The pattern is shaped to a wider curve at the front and is straight at the back. Fold the chiffon in half lengthways along the fold and tack along the seam line. With right sides facing place the chiffon onto the bodice so that the raw edges are aligned. Pin and machine in place. Press the seams away from the neck edge and topstitch to hold the chiffon in place. This topstitching can then form the guide for a row of beads to be sewn on top with a running stitch. Take care not to sew beads where the bodice overlaps at the front and back.

SKIRT

Tack down the centre front lines to transfer the marking to the right side of the skirt and tack around the hem and

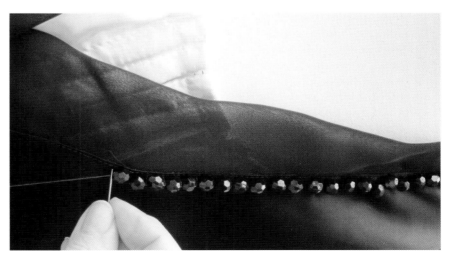

Sew beads along the edge of the chiffon band.

along the top edge for the same purpose. Join the train to either panel by pinning right sides together and machining along the seam lines. Trim the seams with pinking shears and press the seams open. Machine two rows of gathering across the top of the train panel and pull to gather to reduce the top to 3cm. There are two small pleats marked on each skirt panel along the top edge and these can be folded in place and machined across the top, within the seam allowance, to hold in place.

The curved hem of the original skirt is finished by a 7cm bias cut facing. Cut the bias strips to include seam allowance, and press the raw edges in. To help form the curved edges of the hem sew a single row of temporary gathering stich at each curve within the seam allowance of the skirt, pull gently to gather and the seam allowance will begin to curl over; press along the folded edge. With right sides facing pin the facing in place and machine to the dress. The facing is then slipstitched to the back of the satin. Wide black bias binding has been used on the reproduction gown. The facing is sewn to the skirt with a long slipstitch that picks up one thread of the skirt at a time. Press the hem lightly along the edge when sewn to prevent the facing from showing on the right side of the satin.

The chiffon side panels hanging down from the waist are finished with a hand-rolled hem on the original gown. The thread used was not colour fast and so it is now a shade of brown. A rolled-hem foot was attached to the sewing machine to create a narrow hem on the reproduction panels. Pressing the first 10cm over twice makes the process of feeding the slippery chiffon fabric into the rolled-hem foot a little easier. When the panels are completed, using a long machine stitch, sew two rows of gathering stitches within the seam allowance. Pull the two top threads, gather until the panels measure 20cm and then knot the threads at either end.

SCARF

To make the narrow neck scarf begin by sandwiching the shorter panel between the two longer panels with a 0.5cm seam and press open. With right sides facing fold the band in half lengthways, match the seams and pin along the raw edges leaving an opening in the centre of 8cm for turning through. Machine around the edge and trim to 0.5cm, snip off the corners and use a long-handled wooden spoon, or similar, and turn the scarf the right way round. Use a bamboo point turner to make sure the corners are sharp, and press. Close the 8cm gap by pressing the seam allowance inwards, pin and slipstitch by hand. To make the decorative bobbles that hang from the four corners, cut four circles of satin big enough to cover each pompom (I used a large reel of thread as a template). Use a double thread and small stitches to gather each bobble over the pompoms. Join the bobbles to the corners of the scarf with a loose chain stitch 1.5cm long made from three

With right sides facing, pin around the edge of the scarf, leaving a gap in the centre for turning through.

Make the scarf bobbles from pompoms and circles of satin.

strands of embroidery thread. Place a drop of Fray Check over the raw edges.

BEADED BODICE PANELS

Begin by layering the tulle. The original gown has four layers of lighter weight cream tulle, a back layer of stiffer tulle and a top layer of black tulle. I tacked two layers of cream tulle under the outer layer of black together to prevent movement. The other layers were tacked behind once the panel was completed. Place the template behind the net and pin at the corners. Trace the outline of each shape either with an air erasable marker or by tracing with thread. The flower motifs were constructed separately on a piece of black net. The flowers are cut out and then applied to the panel once all other sections are completed.

Beginning with the front panel, place it in an embroidery hoop and adjust so the tension is firm. To sew beads use a beading needle to thread beads onto and then use a small needle to couch the beads in place. Sew the sequins flat using a backstitch. For the swirls around the flowers, thread two beads and one sequin onto a needle and backstitch behind each sequin before repeating. The tension is quite loose for the swirls. The cord is lightly stitched in place using a stab stitch and is couched at the corners. The centre back panel has a smaller opening, so it is not necessary to complete another

Cut around the sequin flower motif with small sharp scissors.

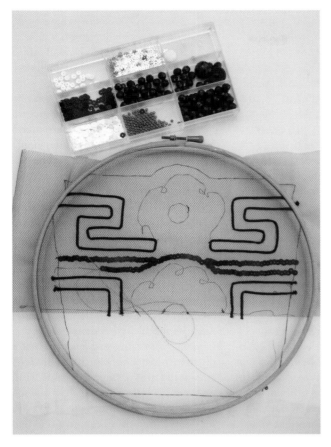

Place the tulle in an embroidery hoop and transfer the lines from the template to the tulle.

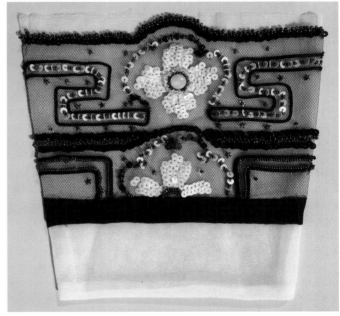

The completed front bib panel.

whole panel, just the section that will show. On the original bodice this is 11cm from the edge of the panel to the top of the chiffon. A folded piece of chiffon has been sewn across the bottom of the beading on the original panel.

Cut a length of chiffon to match the width of the bottom of the beading panel and 5cm wide. Fold in half lengthways. Place the fold along the bottom of the beaded section, pin and slipstitch to the tulle. Finish the long raw edge by folding the edges under and slipstitching to the tulle. To finish the tulle panel trim the seam allowance down to 1cm, fold it behind the panel and slipstitch to the tulle.

BLACK BEADED FLOWER MOTIF ON THE SKIRT

Cut out fifteen pairs of petals, adding seam allowance, and machine around the edge, snip off the point, place a dab of Fray Check at the point and turn the right way round (a chopstick is useful for this process). Make sure the leaf shape is smooth with the seams sitting along the edges, and then press each leaf. Pleat the bottom edge of each leaf into three. Take eight leaves and machine the pleats in place in a continuous strip. Close the circle of leaves by knotting the ends of the thread. Cut two circles of black net that are bigger than the circumference of the hole in the centre and slipstitch the leaves to the net. Place a further leaf in

Feed the ends of the petals through the machine and join in a strip before forming in a circle.

Layer the petals on top of a circle of black net.

rectangles of bugle beads radiate outwards at either side, edged with a further two rows of seed beads. Bugle beads are sewn all around the motif at this stage before being edged with a final row of seed beads. Six faceted beads are sewn along the top of the motif. To make the beaded fringe that hangs from the lower edge of the motif, take a length of narrow bias binding 10cm long and fold in half. The beaded fringe is sewn to the folded edge and the completed section is then sewn behind the motif. Thread a beading needle with a single thread and tie a knot in one end and attach to the centre of the bias strip. Thread nineteen seed beads onto a beading needle and push onto the thread, add a further single bead and then push the needle back through the previous nineteen beads only and backstitch at the top. The other fringes are the same length and are spaced 2mm apart.

the space behind each leaf. Sew a bead at the point of each leaf with a single stitch of double thread, then wind the thread around the base of the bead twice before backstitching at the back of the leaf. Further beads are sewn in random places between the tips of the leaves and the centre. Sew a domed button in the centre of the flower and a row of beads around the button. To do this, thread a line of beads onto a beading needle, enough to sit around the edge of the button, and couch in place with a separate needle and thread.

BELT

The belt is comprised of four shaped beaded sections, for which a pattern has been provided. They sit at the centre front, centre back and at the sides of the waist. There are rectangular sections of beaded net in between the motifs measuring 3.5cm high and 8cm wide. On the original belt, the front motif has a circle of faceted beads in the centre; the three other motifs have a single flat bead sewn in the centre. The beading is sewn onto separate black net sections before being mounted, and then all sections are hand sewn to

a straight satin belt. The reproduction belt has just one beaded motif sewn at the centre front.

To make the beaded motif for the centre front, place the motif template behind a larger rectangle of net and trace the outline onto the net with a white marker pen. The net can then be placed in an embroidery hoop if desired. I found it easier to work on a smaller piece of net which was the motif with a 2cm seam allowance around the edge; the disadvantage with this method is that when beading the cut edges of the net catch the thread.

To make the inner circle of beads, thread a beading needle with a single strand of thread and make a knot in the long end. Then at the edge of the inner circle bring the thread through to the front of the motif and backstitch. Thread eighteen beads onto the beading needle and starting at the outer edge of the circle wind the beads into a spiral and couch in place with a separate needle and thread. Then make the two surrounding circles by threading six black seed beads at a time onto a beading needle and couching every three beads. Two

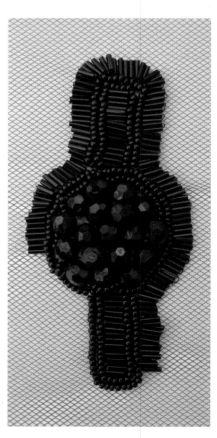

Working from the centre outwards, sew beads to black net to make the motif for the centre front of the belt.

When eleven columns have been made curve the bias tape and sew to the back of the motif so that the fringe hangs down at the front.

To make the satin belt cut a rectangle of fabric long enough to fit around the waist and 9cm wide, which includes 1cm seam allowance. With right sides facing fold the band in half lengthways and pin along the raw edges leaving an opening in the centre of 8cm for turning through. Machine around the edge and trim to 0.5cm, snip off the corners and use a long-handled wooden spoon, or similar, and turn the scarf the right way round. Use a bamboo point turner to make sure the corners are sharp, and press. Close the 8cm gap by pressing the seam allowance inwards, pin and slipstitch by hand. Mark the centre front and centre back and the position of the four motifs. Pin the motifs in place and slipstitch to the belt. The belt is hand stitched to the dress once all sections are in place. The belt fastens at the left-hand side with a triangle comprised of two snap fasteners at the outer edge and a hook and bar sewn behind.

SLEEVES

Begin by hemming the long edges and then inner edges of the point. This is a rolled hem done by hand on the original garment and a rolled hem sewn by machine on the reproduction. To close the seam nearest the body a French seam is used. To make the French seam place wrong sides together and pin and machine along the seam line. Trim to 3mm and press the seam to one side. Turn to the right side and fold in half and press along the seam, encasing the raw edges. Sew a 4mm seam and press to one side. Attach the sleeves to the armhole of the foundation bodice. The sleeve is closed with a backstitch at 22cm down from the fold. Sew the beaded tassels to the four points at the bottom of the sleeves. Pin the sleeves to the armholes of the bodice and machine around the seam line; finish the edges by cutting with pinking shears. The seam is pushed into the bodice.

ASSEMBLING THE GOWN

Put the foundation bodice and attached underskirt on the stand, fasten and gather the bodice to fit by adjusting the cotton tape at the centre back. The line tacked around the lower section of the bodice is the guide for adding all parts of the body of the gown. Place the chiffon layers at the sides of the skirt and pin in place. Join the over bodice to the skirt at the waist and put on the stand with the right side wrapping over the left, over the foundation bodice. The flower motif is sewn to the dress from behind using a double thread and large stitches to enable it to be removed when the dress is in storage. The flower motif is positioned at the bottom of the overlap of the skirt when the dress is on the stand. The skirt is joined to the false front with two swing catches, each 2.5cm long, at the hem. Finally add the belt, hooks and eyes, and snap fasteners.

ADAPTING THE EVENING GOWN

If the gown is to be worn repeatedly for a stage play the foundation bodice could be made from a stronger fabric such as coutil. The beaded belt could be replaced by a satin belt that fastens with a decorative buckle. The dress has many layers that could be left off or altered. The centre front and centre back tulle panels could be replaced with black lace backed with white silk. The sleeves and chiffon skirt panels could be removed and the foundation skirt lengthened to make a version of the dress similar to the illustration by Ida Pritchard used at the start of this chapter.

Assemble the evening gown on the stand.

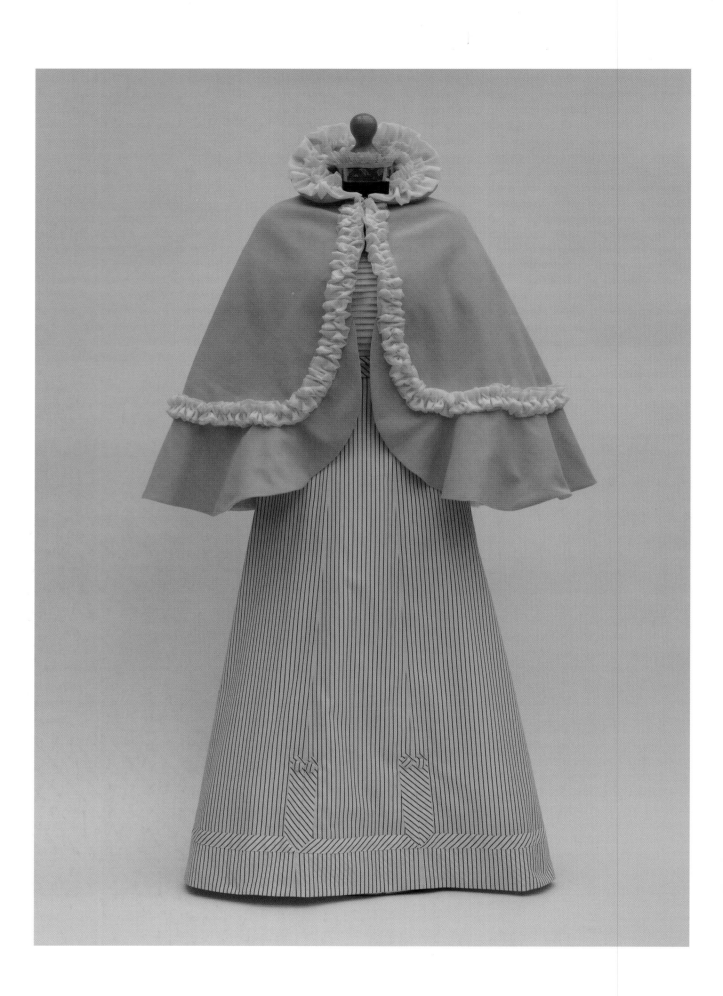

Chapter 10
Lined Cape

'The cutting of capes is a very simple matter. They must be properly balanced to secure the fullness falling in folds that will hang gracefully', stated Edwardian Ladies' Tailoring *in 1910. In the same period* The Lady's World *showed designs for three short summer capes with the recommended fabrics being silk, velvet or chiffon. It was suggested each cape could be mounted 'upon a plain lining of silk'. The yellow cape featured in this chapter is from Royal Pavilion & Museums, Brighton & Hove, museum accession number C003367.3. It is a half-circular cape made from a silk grosgrain fabric with layered organza and chiffon ruffles around the front edge and along the seam between the cape and the flounce that passes around the hem of the cape. It was purchased by Katherine Farebrother from Dickins and Jones, a smart London department store, in c.1900 along with a coordinating long gown. Although the cape has the appearance of being a decorative and*

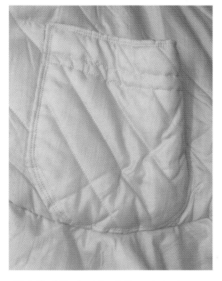

Detail of the inside of the original cape showing the patch pocket.

MATERIALS AND EQUIPMENT

3.5 metres yellow silk grosgrain fabric, or similar
2 metres yellow chiffon
2 metres white chiffon
Three sets of size 3 silver hooks and eyes
1 metre lightweight wadding or batting
1 metre domette interlining fabric
3.5 metres ivory habutai lining
20cm collar canvas
Thread
Sewing machine
Bamboo point turner
Rouleau loop turner (optional)

frivolous garment, it is in fact also a practical one. Inside it has a quilted, padded lining for warmth, and a roomy and useful patch pocket.

It fastens edge to edge at the centre front with three sets of hooks and eyes. The collar is rounded at the front edge and has ruffles on the top and bottom, which suggests that it could be worn either flat to the body or pulled upwards and worn as a high collar. Edwardian fashion journalists such as Mrs Pritchard, writing in *The Ladies' Field*, stressed the importance of clothing that was 'becoming' to the complexion, the face and the figure, suggesting that this collar could have been used to softly frame the face of the wearer. *Weldon's Practical Needlework* wrote in more specific terms about the advantages of frilling around a collar, stating: 'it gives the look of fluffiness and fullness that a thin neck needs.'

An illustration of the front of the finished cape. (Royal Pavilion & Museums, Brighton & Hove)

The original cape with the collar turned up.

Left: The reproduction cape.

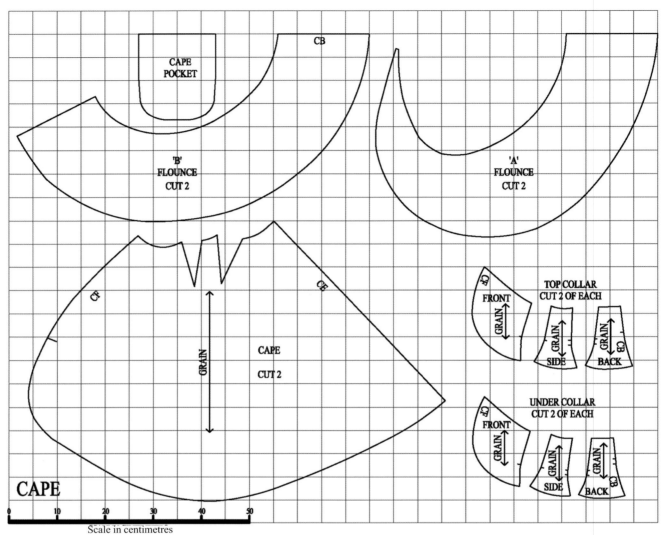

Cape pattern.

Enlarge the pattern, add seam allowance and use it to cut and make a toile to test the shape and fit of the cape before cutting in fabric.

Cutting

Place the pattern on the fabric; by following the grain line indicated on the pattern, the centre back will be cut on the bias. Use tailor's chalk to draw around the outline of the pattern and then transfer the shape to the other side of the fabric by placing carbon paper underneath and wheeling around the edge with a tracing wheel. Add a generous seam allowance. Transfer pattern markings for the darts and

other balance points to the fabric using tailor's tacks. Use the upper cape pattern to cut two pieces of wadding but do not add seam allowance. Cut into the darts and remove the V shape of each dart; the wadding sits edge to edge rather than darts being sewn in the bulky wadding. Cut canvas for the under collar and add seam allowance.

The flounce is cut in sections with the centre back sitting on the bias. The lining is cut from the same pattern pieces as the cape and needs seam allowance; a single layer of domette should also be cut from the flounce pattern pieces. The top and bottom collar pieces are cut from the same fabric and also need seam allowance.

The bottom collar pieces also need collar canvas cut using the pattern pieces, with added seam allowance. Use carbon paper and a tracing wheel to transfer markings to all pieces of the collar canvas.

The ruffles are cut from strips measuring the width of the fabric, which is 150cm. The yellow strips are 12cm deep and the upper, white strips are 10cm deep, which includes 0.5cm seam allowance. A total of five ruffles are needed to sew around the cape and a further length is needed if a ruffle is required for the under collar. Further strips are needed for the upper collar. A yellow ruffle sits around the outer edge, which should be cut 16cm deep, to be

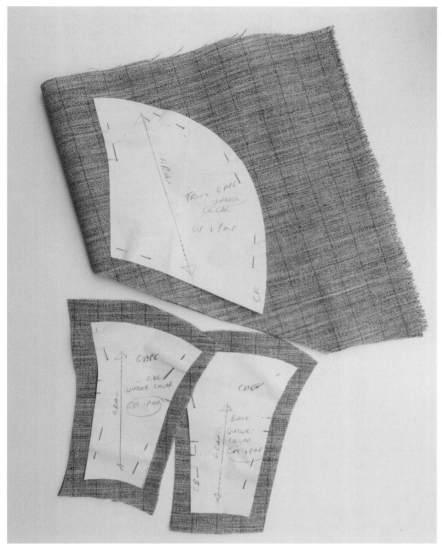

Cut the collar canvas and add seam allowance.

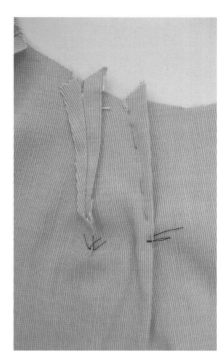

Form the darts in the cape, cut and press open.

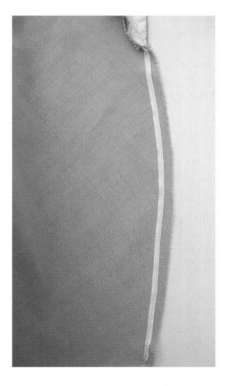

Sew narrow tape to the inside of the seam allowance.

folded to 8cm. A small white ruffle that sits near the neck measures 10cm in total and 5cm when folded. Cut the pocket and add seam allowance; cut a further pocket lining section from the same fabric.

Making order

The outer cape

Separate all pieces and begin by joining the centre back seam. Place right sides together and pin and machine along the seam line. Press the seam open. To form the darts, working on the wrong side of the fabric fold the dart down the centre, pin in place and machine from the wide end to the point. Cut away excess fabric to make open darts and press flat. To prevent the neck from stretching machine a row of stay stitching using a small machine stitch, within the seam allowance. To prevent the centre front sections from stretching machine a narrow cotton tape on the reverse side just to the inside of the seam allowance.

Flounce

Mount the lining sections of the flounce by placing a layer of domette on the reverse side of each piece. Use large basting stitches to hold the domette to the lining, making sure that the layers are lying flat. This will help to give a smooth finish. Seam the lining sections together and press the seams to one side. Seam the outer flounce sections together and press the seams open. Working on a large flat surface, lay the flounce with the right side facing upwards and lay the lining on top so that the right sides are facing. Lay all seams on top of each other and pin in place around the bottom edge only, along the seam line. Machine around the edge, trim the seam allowance down to 1cm and snip into the seam allowance at intervals to give the flounce a smooth curved edge. Turn the right way round and press. Lay the finished flounce back on the flat surface and pin and tack the top raw edge together, smoothing the lining upwards as you go.

Attach the flounce to the bottom of the cape with right sides facing and raw edges aligned. Line up the centre back seam and push a long pin through both seams – this can be kept in place while sewing to make sure the seams match perfectly. Pin and tack the flounce in place and machine along the seam line. Press the seam towards the inside of the cape.

Collar

To make the collar, begin by laying the collar canvas on the reverse side of the under collar pieces and then secure in place by tacking along the seam lines. With right sides facing pin all under collar pieces together along the seam lines and machine. Trim the collar canvas by cutting close to the line of stitching. Trim the collar seams and snip at intervals to allow the seams to sit smoothly once pressed. Press the collar over a tailor's ham or similar. Pin and machine the upper collar sections together, trim the seam allowances and press the seams open.

To join the upper and under collar place right sides together and pin and machine around the top edge; the bottom edge is left free for joining to the cape. Layer the seam allowance to avoid a bulky seam and snip at intervals. Turn the right way round and press along the edge (use the bamboo point turner to push the seam outwards). Check that both edges of the collar are the same size by folding it in half, and adjust if necessary. To finish, sew a temporary row of tacking around the top edge of the collar.

Ruffles

The ruffles edging the original cape are self-faced double ruffles made from long strips folded into three and gathered in the centre. On the original cape they are made by hand and joined to the cape with a small running stitch down the centre of each ruffle. The reproduction ruffles are made by folding each strip in half lengthways and machining a 0.5cm seam. A rouleau loop turner is useful for turning the ruffles the right way round or a safety pin can be attached to one end and pushed through. To form the ruffles pin one yellow strip to a firm surface such as an ironing board or cork board with the seam lying in the centre and underneath. Place a white strip on top and centre it so that an equal band of yellow is visible along either edge. Take a long needle, threaded with white double thread, tie a knot and sew a backstitch and then sew a running stitch down the centre with stitches approximately 1cm long. When reaching the end pull the thread to gather the ruffle strip, distributing the gathers evenly while pulling until the ruffle measures 60cm. Fasten the thread with a backstitch. The ruffles are attached to the cape by hand because a machine stitch would make them look too stiff. To attach the ruffles to the cape, place the cape on a stand and pin the ruffles in place around the cape following the edge of the upper cape.

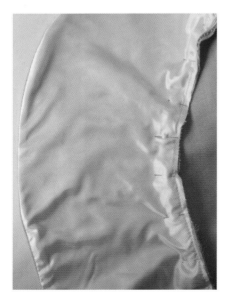

Pin and machine the flounce to the edge of the cape.

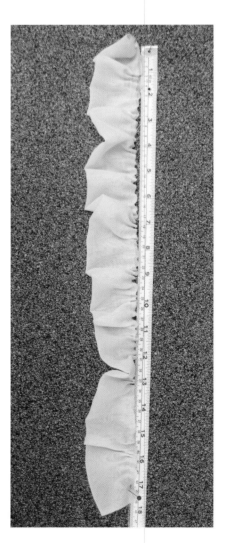

The length of the frill can be accurately checked by pinning it to a cork board alongside a tape measure.

Place pins horizontally and turn the raw edges of the ruffles under as you go. Once all ruffles are in place sew in place with a double thread and long back stitches.

The lower collar ruffles can be added before the collar is attached to the cape. The upper collar ruffles should be pinned in place with the cape on the stand once the collar has been securely sewn in place. The collar has the same ruffles as the edge of the cape sewn on the under collar, this should be done before the top collar has its ruffles attached.

The top collar has a slightly different type of ruffle. Cut a width of white chiffon 32mm deep and fold in half lengthways and sew a 0.5cm seam. Turn the right way round and, with the seam lying in the centre and underneath, place pins across the width of the strip. Take a long needle, threaded with white double thread, tie a knot and sew a backstitch and then sew a running stitch down the centre with stitches approximately 1cm long. When you reach the end, fold the strip in half lengthways and pull the thread to gather, distributing the gathers evenly while pulling until the ruffle will sit along the top edge of the collar.

Cut a final fabric width of yellow chiffon and fold in half lengthways and machine a 0.5cm seam, then turn the right way round. Flatten the strip so that the seam runs along one edge. With the long needle threaded with white double thread, tie a knot and sew a backstitch and then sew a running stitch down the edge of the seam with stitches approximately 1cm long. Pull to gather. The top collar ruffles are pinned in place so that the gathered edges are resting up against each other. Slipstitch in place.

Quilted lining

To make the quilted lining, first mark the lines for quilting on the right side of the lining. Use an air erasable marker to mark the quilting lines, which are 6cm apart and run diagonally at right angles to the centre back. The lining sections are quilted

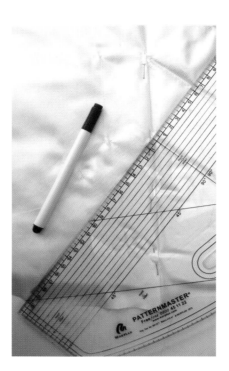

Mark chevrons on top of the lining using an air erasable marker and Pattern Master.

separately before being joined together. To make up the quilted lining place the layer of lightweight wadding on a flat surface and place the lining piece on top; baste together with large stitches. Machine the quilting lines making sure that each line is sewn in the same direction to prevent the fabric from puckering. The lining may have moved during the quilting process so place the pattern piece back on top of the quilted pieces and re-mark if necessary. Join the centre back seam, taking care to match the chevrons created by the quilting. Tack the wadding to the fabric around the darts in the lining and pin and machine the darts in place, sewing from the wide end to the point. Press flat from the right side of the cape. Before attaching the lining to the cape, fold the centre front openings to the inside along the seam line and press along the folded edge. Tack and herringbone lightly to the cape taking care not to let the stitches show on the right side.

The hooks and eyes are sandwiched between the cape and the lining and so need to be sewn on before the lining is

attached. They are spaced 6cm apart with the first set of hooks and eyes starting 1.5cm down from the neck seam line. Sew the hooks and eyes in place, beginning with a hook on the right hand side and alternating with a bar before a final hook. Sew corresponding fastenings on the other side.

Patch pocket

To make the patch pocket, first mount each section with domette, which will help to give a smooth finish. Then with right sides facing join the pocket lining to the pocket along the straight edge leaving a gap of 6cm for turning through. Press the seam and press lightly along the fold that forms the top of the pocket. With right sides facing, pin around the edge of the pocket and machine along the seam line. Snip off the top corners and clip around the curved edge at 1cm intervals. Turn the pocket the right way round by pulling through the opening. Use a bamboo point turner to push the corners out and to make sure the edge is crisp. Press lightly and then close the gap by slipstitching by hand. The pocket on the original cape is not quilted but has 3cm wide diagonal lines of machining following in the same direction as on the cape. Place the pocket on top of the right front cape lining and position it 17cm in from the front edge with the bottom edge resting just above the seam line. On the museum's cape the pocket is slipstitched around the edge; it can, however, be topstitched to the lining by machine on the reproduction cape.

Finishing

To add the lining to the cape, lie the cape on a flat surface with the wrong side facing upwards. Lay the lining on top with the right side facing upwards and line up the centre back seam and darts, pin in place all around the edge and through the centre back seam. Fold the edge of the lining under and pin and tack to the edge of the cape. Smooth the lining upwards towards the

Add a hanging loop to the centre back neck.

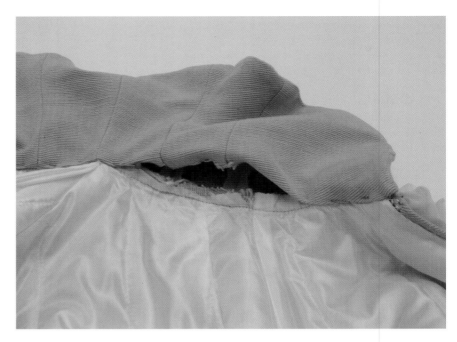

Machine the under collar to the outer neck edge and slipstitch the upper collar to the lining.

neck edge and pin along the seam allowance at the neck edge. To test that the lining is not pulling, place the cape on a dress stand or on a person. If the cape is hanging smoothly then slipstitch the lining to the cape around the edge.

There is a hanging loop at the centre back neck made from a rouleau loop. To make the loop, cut a strip of lining fabric on the bias 3cm x 20cm. Fold in half lengthways and machine 0.5cm away from the fold, pulling the bias strip as you sew. Trim the seam allowance down to 0.2mm. To turn the right way round, insert the rouleau loop turner, catch the top and pull. Press before forming into a loop measuring 9cm. Place the raw edges into the centre back seam allowance and machine the loop in place.

To attach the collar match up the centre back marks and with right sides facing pin the under collar around the edge of the neck, keeping the top collar out of the way. Tack in place and then

Place the cape on a stand and pin the frill around the edge of the upper collar.

machine along the seam line with the collar on the top as you sew. Trim and grade the seam allowance and then snip into the seam allowance. Press the seams into the collar over a tailor's ham or a sleeve board and fold the bottom raw edge of the top collar under and pin and hand sew to the lining using a

ADAPTING THE CAPE

To adapt the cape for daywear a wool or serge fabric could be used and the ruffles could be omitted. The quilted lining can be removed and a cotton mounting fabric used instead. The cape could also be made in black satin with black lace ruffles or guipure motifs, and black silk cord ties for glamorous evening wear. To adapt the cape for a quick change just one hook and bar can be used.

small felling stitch. Add the large white collar ruffle around the edge of the upper collar and sew in place with a small running stitch. Finally add the narrower single yellow ruffle to slightly overlap and sew in place with a small running stitch.

Chapter 11
Evening Bag, Hat and Parasol

An Edwardian ensemble was incomplete without the addition of a range of accessories and many possible candidates in the museums' archives were considered for reproduction in this chapter. The three projects were selected because it was possible to source similar fabrics and trimmings and because it was possible to adapt them to a range of other styles.

The small drawstring bag was a useful yet elegant addition to evening wear for an Edwardian woman. Described in advertising and editorial features as either a 'Dorothy bag' or by the French term réticule, they were made from silk or velvet and were either encrusted with beads, sequins or tassels, or sometimes all three. A crocheted or macramé version was also available for day use and craft manuals and journals featured many examples for readers to make. Worthing Museum has a small purple velvet Dorothy bag adorned with a floral trellis pattern around the outside with a central floral motif, formed from Berlin steel beadwork. Dorothy bags were available to purchase at department stores but dressmakers could also make their own versions.

Millinery was a highly specialized occupation and Edwardian women had a wide choice of skilled milliners to visit when a new hat was needed. They also had the option of making their own hat by following patterns and instructions that were supplied in dressmaking manuals and journals. The parasol featured in this section is quite fancy but for a woman on a lower income an unlined parasol covered in a striped canvas fabric was a fashionable accessory and a practical sunshade for a walk in the park on Sundays.

Postcard of a woman carrying a striped parasol and wearing a walking suit and feather boa. (Private collection)

DRAWSTRING BEADED EVENING BAG

The bag featured in this chapter comes from Royal Pavilion & Museums, Brighton & Hove, Leeson and Vokins sub-collection, museum accession number CTTMP000277. Although the bag is undated it is a style that can be seen in journals and dressmaking manuals throughout the Edwardian period. The original bag is made from black grosgrain satin with a dull sheen and is fully lined with black silk. There is a densely beaded exterior section on both sides of the bag comprised of

flowers, hearts and abstract swirls. The top edge is scalloped and edged with two rows of black beads. A casing on the outside is threaded with silk cord, which is finished off at either end by round beaded bobbles. Due to the weight of the glass beads the bag feels heavy but it is also robust and in excellent condition. The reproduction bag is beaded on one side only and features a simplified version of the beading pattern designed and beaded by Rachel Woolcott.

The original beaded evening bag from Leeson and Vokins department store, Brighton. (Royal Pavilion & Museums)

Detail of the bottom of the original beaded evening bag.

Left: The reproduction accessory projects.

MATERIALS AND EQUIPMENT

25cm Duchess silk
25cm lining
25g x 8/0 silver lined chocolate rocaille beads for the main swirl and hearts
25g x 7mm bugles col.1870 Gütermann to fill the flowers
25g seed beads col.1480 Gütermann to outline the flowers
25g x 8/0 black rocaille beads for edging
40 x 0.5cm bright gold balls
2.2 metres x 3mm black lacing cord
Embroidery hoop
Beading needles
Thread
Fray Check

Cutting

Copy the pattern from the book and cut around the edge. Do not add seam allowance at this stage. Place the fabric face down on a flat surface, layer carbon paper face down on top and finally the template facing upwards. Use a small tracing wheel to transfer the pattern onto the reverse side of the bag. Thread mark to transfer the marking to the front of the bag. Cut the lining using the same pattern, and add 1.5cm seam allowance around the outside.

Making order

Each bead on the reproduction bag was sewn on individually with a running stitch. They could also be sewn by the couching method, which involves threading a few beads at a time onto the beading needle and using a second short needle and thread to catch the beads and thread down, either behind every bead or every few beads. To begin beading the bag, place the marked bag section in an embroidery hoop with the right side of the fabric facing upwards. Using a beading needle and single thread start with a knot and backstitch on the reverse side of the fabric and start beading the inside of the flower shapes with bugle beads. Fill the flower with two bugle beads in each petal and complete the flowers by outlining with a further shape of bugle beads. Form the long swirling shapes and heart shapes by sewing three long rows of seed beads next to each other. Finally, randomly scatter and individually sew on the bright gold balls. Repeat the beading pattern on the other bag piece if desired.

Once the beading is complete the

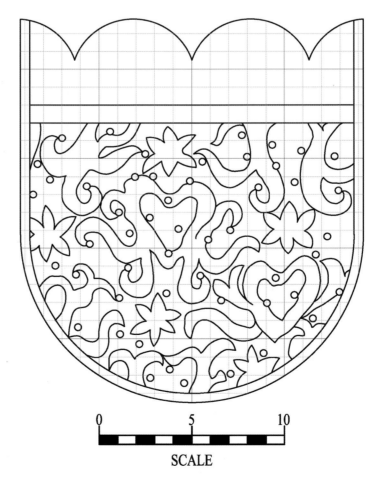

0　　　　　　5　　　　　　10

SCALE

Evening bag pattern.

Transfer the markings to the wrong side of the fabric using a tracing wheel and carbon paper.

Pin the casing to the front of the bag.

Sew beads along the top of the casing.

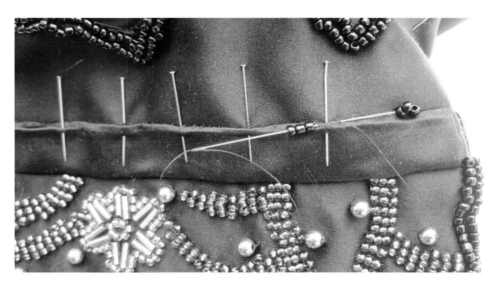

next stage is to add the casings on the outside of the bag for the cord to pass through. The rectangular casings are cut on the straight grain and measure 20cm x 3.5cm. Press all edges of the casings under by 1cm. With right sides facing place the seam line of the casing piece along the top row of beads and pin in place. Attach a zipper foot to the

machine and machine along the seam line. Making sure the raw edges are still folded inwards, sew the top edge of the casing in place and hand sew the top of the casing using a small needle and felling stitch. Repeat on the other bag piece. The next stage is to sew a row of small black beads along the top of the casings. Thread three beads onto the

beading needle and make a backstitch to form a small pyramid effect. Leave a space of 13mm between each pyramid.

Before joining both bag pieces together trim the excess fabric away to leave a 1.5cm seam allowance around the bag. With right sides facing place the bag pieces together and pin through the seam lines. Still using the

A long cord strap is made from a piece of cord measuring 110cm. Fold the cord in half and tie a knot in the end leaving a loop measuring 4cm. Place the raw ends inside the bag and pin in place at the side seams 5cm down from the top edge of the bag, and oversew to secure. Thread a single cord measuring 55cm through each casing and join the cords together by forming a knot at either end. Trim the frayed ends and hand sew over the edges. The knots on the original evening bag are covered in small black beads and this process can be done at this stage if required. To close the bag hold the knots at either end of the cord threaded through the casing and pull the cords.

With right sides facing slot the bag into the lining.

Slipstitch the bottom of the lining.

zipper foot, machine carefully around the edge with the needle positioned to the left, lifting the foot and pivoting when necessary to prevent the fabric from dragging. Trim the seams and snip at intervals. Join the lining seams at the sides, leaving the bottom curved edge open by 5cm for turning the bag out. With right sides facing position the lining over the bag and match up the raw edges along the top and the side seams.

Pin and machine along the scalloped edge, using the zipper foot; leave the needle in the fabric and pivot the bag when you reach a dip in the scallops. Trim the scalloped edge down to 0.5cm and snip into the curves and into the points of the scallop. Dab Fray Check onto the scallop points and allow to dry. Turn the right way round by pulling through the gap in the bottom of the lining. Finish the beading by sewing two rows of black seed beads down the sides at the front of the side seam to form a continuous row all around the edge of the bag. To close the lining gap slipstitch by hand.

ADAPTING THE BAG

The Dorothy bag can be made to coordinate with an outfit by using the same fabric. A variety of floral patterns can be sewn to the outside either with embroidery stitches or by beading. Collector Marion May has a black silk drawstring bag decorated on both sides with small fuchsias and roses made from coloured net.

The reproduction evening bag showing the position of the cord.

VELVET TOQUE

The velvet hat chosen for this chapter is from Worthing Museum and is described as a toque, which is a turban or beret style, mostly brimless hat. The museum accession number is 1966/860. The hat was made by R. Sayle & Co., Cambridge, and is dated *c.*1912. It is made from mushroom brown cotton velvet and is lined inside with black silk. The hat is constructed over a domed cage shaped with millinery wire. The crown is covered by ruched velvet and the brim is separately covered with pleated velvet. The decoration across the front of the brim is made from a band of black net

Front view of the original museum hat. (Worthing Museum and Art Gallery)

MATERIALS AND EQUIPMENT

Decorative braid
75cm **x** 25cm black net
1 ball of Wendy Roam Fusion 4ply wool
Fine gold thread
1 metre **x** 2cm antique gold lace braid
Inks and a paintbrush for adding shading to the braid
Craft glue (optional)
Embroidery hoop
Hand sewing needles
Hat
1 metre lightweight brown cotton velvet
25cm black lining
50cm **x** 1cm black ribbon
3 metres **x** 1.2mm cotton-covered millinery wire
Strong thread for securing the millinery wire frame
Pliers
Sticky tape
Thread
Tailor's chalk
Sewing machine
A hat block (useful but not essential)
Silk rose

The reproduction hat.

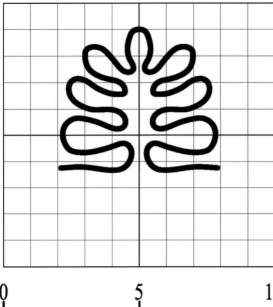

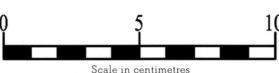

0   5   10

Scale in centimetres

Leaf motif template.

decorated with a wavy pattern resembling autumn leaves. The leaf motifs are made from wool and gold thread with a further and larger wave of antique gold lace winding between them. A large dusky pink rose adorns the left side of the hat. The rose is made from velvet and organza with pale yellow tipped stamens with dark green velvet leaves placed behind.

The reproduction hat is a close copy of the original hat although it has been made larger around the circumference of the head at 57cm; the original hat measures just 47cm. The silk rose would not have been produced by a dressmaker and therefore instructions have not been included for reproducing it, although details of the supplier are given at the end of the book.

Cutting

Cut a long strip of velvet on the bias to cover the brim, 125cm long and 18cm wide. Cut an oval of velvet on the bias, 68cm long and 56cm wide, to cover the crown. Cut a rectangle of lining 60cm x 18cm and a further circle approximately 7cm in diameter.

Making order

MILLINERY WIRE FRAME

Begin by straightening the millinery wire using thumbs and fingers; this will prevent the wire from distorting once made up into the frame. The millinery wire frame is formed of three oval shapes joined together by strengthening struts – the crown, the head size and the brim. The head size is the circumference of the head plus ease.

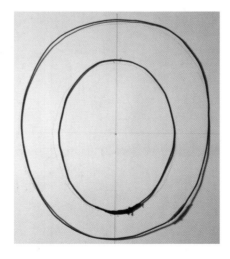

Make the millinery wire ovals using a template drawn on paper.

Make a pencil diagram on paper showing the dimensions of the measurement taken from around the head (head size), the crown and the brim. The head size measurement used for the reproduction hat is 57cm or $22^1/_2$ inches, which is the average size for a hat. Position the head size in the centre and mark centre front and centre back. The brim is 7cm deep at the centre front and narrows to 4cm at the centre back. The crown measures slightly less than the head size at 52cm. Use these ellipses as a template to form the wire frame for the head size, crown and brim. Use the pliers to cut the millinery wire to the correct size.

Join each oval by overlapping the edges by 3cm. Cover the join with sticky tape and then wrap with strong thread or embroidery thread. To make the struts that join all three ovals together make a small L shape at the end of the millinery wire and place alongside the inside of the brim at the centre front. Measure 8cm and form another L, which is joined to the centre front of the head size. Then form the centre back strut, which measures 4cm, and add two further struts to fit at the sides. Form the crown as a cage with two wire arches at right angles (crossed at the crown) connecting the brim to the crown piece. The crown is 11cm high. Use thread to bind the joins between the wire hoops and the spokes of wire radiating outwards. Bind all the joins with sticky tape and then wrap securely with thread.

The next process is to cover the frame with net. Cut the crown tip piece first,

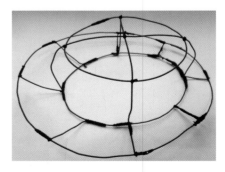

Make the cage for the hat.

Cover the cage with net and bind the edge of the brim.

much as possible. As the brim gets narrower at the back of the hat, there will be excess fabric along the edge, which can be trimmed away.

CROWN

To form the crown take the large oval of velvet, cut on the bias, and mark the exact centre of the oval with tailor's chalk. Mark a smaller oval in the centre slightly larger than the dimensions of the oval used to form the crown of the wire frame. Taper the outer corners outwards slightly to make them more pointed (like the shape of an eye). Outline this shape with two parallel rows of gathering stitch 1.5cm apart. Use these threads to make a gently ruched shape at the centre of the fabric, and tie the ends of the threads in a knot to secure.

Run a gathering stitch around the edge of the fabric oval all the way round, 1cm in from the raw edge. Using the threads from these stitches, gather the fabric to form a domed shape with a ruched section at the crown. Ease the fabric shape over the wire frame, positioning it with the one of the V shapes at either side of the crown section pointing towards the centre front. Distribute the folds of velvet as evenly as possible, and gather to fit snugly around. Stitch as

exactly to fit the oval of wire, and oversew the raw edge onto the wire. Cover the brim in the same way but leave a 1.5cm allowance around the inside of the head-size band and clip the curves to help this piece fit to the wire. This will fold upwards inside the hat to begin to form the band. Oversew the edge of the net onto the wire. Cut a rectangle of net long enough to lap the sides of the crown, approximately 59cm and as tall at the hat (11cm) and cover the sides. Use a 1.5cm wide strip of calico cut on the cross to bind the edge of the brim all the way round, stab stitching closer to the raw edge than to the wire. The binding should be taut and smooth and disguise all the joins between the bits of wire.

BRIM

To cover the brim, begin by running a long gathering stitch along both long edges of the velvet strip (alternating a longer stitch on the wrong side, short stitch on the right side of the fabric). Seam the short ends of the strip together to make a continuous loop, and mark halfway along the length of the strip with a pin. This will be the centre front of the brim, and the seam will be positioned at the back. Fold the loop in half lengthways with wrong

sides facing. Using the gathering threads, ease the velvet band around the brim, ruching up the fabric and distributing the folds as evenly as possible. The brim will be sandwiched or enclosed with the fabric, with the fold along the outer edge of the brim and the raw edges at the innermost edge. Stab stitch the fabric into place on the wire frame, keeping stitches hidden among the folds of velvet as

Add the brim cover.

Gather the crown by sewing double rows of running stitches in an ellipse.

Add the lining to the inside of the hat.

inconspicuously as possible to the brim, over the edge of the velvet covering the brim, folding under and enclosing all raw edges.

MAKING THE LINING

Along one long edge, fold and press a 0.5cm hem. Along the other long edge, fold, press and stitch a 1.5cm hem, which will be the casing for the ribbon drawstring. Fold in half widthways with right sides together, and pin the short sides together. You will now have a cylinder. Stitch this seam, leaving the end with the drawstring casing open, and thread the ribbon through the casing and draw the ribbons to gather the tip, and tie in a knot.

Take the 7cm lining circle and apply fusible interfacing to the reverse side. Glue or stitch this inside the crown of the hat at the apex of the crown. Position the lining inside the hat, with the seam at the centre back. Pin the lining fabric to the velvet at the inside edge of the brim around the head-fit band, easing in any fullness. Slipstitch into position. Adjust the drawstring if necessary. The hat is now ready for trimming.

DECORATIVE BRAID

To make the decorative braid that runs across the brim, take a single piece of black net. Press the net with a steam iron and a pressing cloth if needed. Thread mark a rectangle in the centre of the net measuring 70cm x 6cm, leaving a border around the edges. Trace off or print the leaf motif. Join the leaf motifs together ensuring that every other leaf faces upwards. Place the template behind the net and pin to an ironing board or cork board. Use the white marker pen to trace around each leaf shape. The leaf motif is formed by lightly couching two strands of wool around the outline of each leaf. This is a tricky process and it might be easier to use a craft glue to stick the wool in place before couching. To form the motifs, cut a long piece of wool, approximately 1 metre long and fold in half. Place two strands of wool over the outline and use a small needle and a single thread to stitch the wool to the

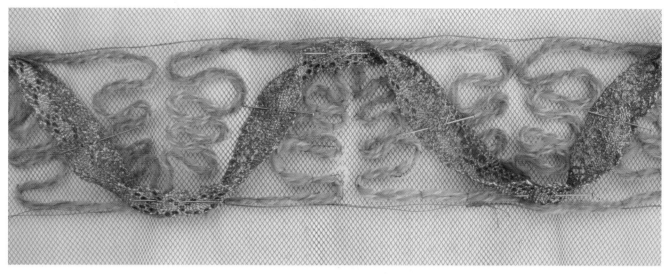

Make the hat braid by couching wool on net, following the shape of the leaf motif.

ADAPTING THE HAT

Women from across all classes of Edwardian society wore hats and this particular hat shape could be dressed up or down. A simpler version could be made without the braid trim and with the addition of a small bunch of violets at one side rather than the rose. A more elaborate version could be made in silk velvet with the addition of a plume of feathers and silk and velvet flowers. The hat brim could also be widened by constructing a larger brim from millinery wire. Writing in *The Ladies' Field*, 3 February, 1906, the fashion journalist 'Penelope' suggested improving a toque with the addition of a 'soft diaphanous veil, draped around the shape and floating behind.'

net. Use a light tension. A fine gold thread is couched on top to finish the motifs. Pin the wider gold braid in a wave pattern between the leaves and hand sew in place with a small running stitch. When finished trim the braid down to the tacked line.

FINISHING THE HAT
Pin the braid across the front of the brim and slipstitch in place. Oversew the flower in place using a double thread.

LACE-TRIMMED PARASOL

The parasol recreated in this section is based on a lace-trimmed parasol from the collection at Worthing Museum, museum accession number 2008/341.

The reproduction parasol.

The museum has several fine examples of parasols wrapped in acid-free tissue paper and stored in large flat drawers in the archive. The examples at the museum are fully lined, or where the fabric has disintegrated it is possible to see where the lining was once attached. Edwardian parasols at the higher end of the market were often highly decorated with lace, ribbons, ruffles and frills and were often made to accessorize a specific outfit. One such

Small black lace parasol with mauve silk lining, mauve grosgrain ribbon tied around the ferrule and an ivory stick. (Worthing Museum and Art Gallery)

Detail of the original parasol handle with silk cord looped around the stick.

The end of the original parasol handle painted with a portrait of a young woman.

example at Worthing Museum is a small black lace-covered parasol with a carved ivory stick, which is lined with mauve silk and finished with a grosgrain ribbon tied around the ferrule.

The parasol chosen for this chapter has a ceramic ball at the end of the handle featuring a handpainted portrait of a young woman wearing a Georgian style dress. This has not been attempted in the reproduction parasol. A cream silk decorative tassel is looped around the lower end of the long wooden stick and could easily be undone and used to wrap around the parasol and use as a tie when not in use. Ten layers of embroidered ivory cotton lace are layered down the parasol, each layer slightly overlapping the one below. The layers are sewn to the parasol with small running stitches. The lace is also caught down in vertical lines at approximately 6cm intervals,

Cutting

If using the parasol kit make a pattern by drawing an inverted T shape on pattern paper using a set square. The horizontal line measures 25cm and the vertical line is 42cm. At the tip of the vertical line square out by 2mm on either side then join the points to form a triangle. The vertical line forms the grain line. If using a different parasol frame, make a triangular pattern by measuring across the space between the spokes, find the midpoint and use a set square to square upwards. Make sure both sides of the triangle are the same shape. Add 1.5cm seam allowance around each side. Cut out enough triangles to complete the parasol; for the kit version ten triangles are needed. The museum's parasol is completely lined and so if making an exact copy then a further ten triangles are needed.

Making order

The reproduction parasol is not lined and therefore the seams are French seams. If a lining is added then the

Inside the original parasol showing the cotton lining.

which would have kept the lace in place when the parasol was folded and held upside down by the handle. A wide taffeta ribbon is tied around the tip of the parasol, known as the ferrule. The parasol is fully lined in plain cotton fabric and so would have been effective as a sunshade.

The reproduction parasol has been made using a parasol kit, which is supplied with a basic frame, handle, stick and separate ferrule. A reproduction parasol could also be made by unpicking the cover from an existing parasol or umbrella and using the cover as a template.

MATERIALS AND EQUIPMENT

Adult parasol kit (*see* list of suppliers)
14m x 5cm lace
1 metre ivory cotton fabric (2 metres if lined)
Thread
50cm x 5.5cm wide satin or taffeta ribbon
PVA craft glue
1 readymade cord with tassels

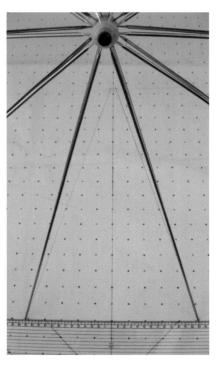

Make a pattern for the reproduction parasol.

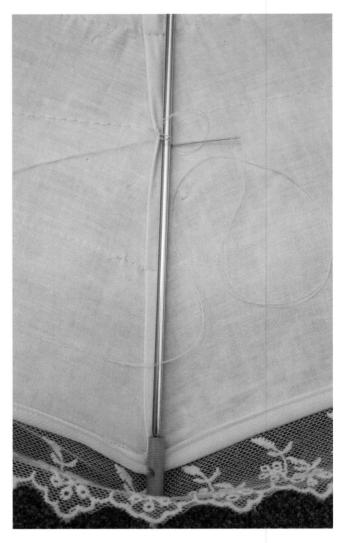

Machine the lace onto the cover.

Hand sew the cover to the frame.

triangles can be joined with a single seam. The following instructions are given for an unlined parasol. To make a French seam place wrong sides together and machine a 1cm seam so that the raw edges show on the right side of the parasol. Trim the seam allowance away close to the line of stitching. Press the seam to one side and then fold along the seam with the raw edges enclosed inside. Pin and machine a 0.5cm seam. Press the French seams to one side. Before adding the lace, check that the parasol cover is a snug fit by pinning the cover to the frame. If the cover fits remove it from the frame and turn the bottom

hem twice and machine a narrow seam. Lay the cover on a flat surface with the right side facing upwards. The first layer of lace hangs over the edge of the parasol. Take the lace and place the raw edge along the top of the seam and pin in place, adding a tiny pleat at the corner of each triangle if needed, as the lace winds around the parasol.

To pin the subsequent layers of lace in place, the cover needs to be placed back on the parasol. Pinning lace around a large parasol is a time-consuming process and best tackled in short bursts. The lace on the original parasol would have been attached in this way, with each layer being sewn

with a small running stitch. The lace on the reproduction parasol has been machined in place. When all layers are in place, using a needle and double thread sew a row of gathering stitches in the seam line at the top of the parasol cover and leave long ends for gathering. Tie a strong knot and firmly sew the tips to the ends of the French seams on the parasol cover using a double thread and backstitch a few times. Place the parasol cover over the frame and line up the seams with the ribs. Slip the ends of the ribs into the tips. Loosely sew the ribs to the French seams about halfway up the frame. Place the handle on the end of the stick

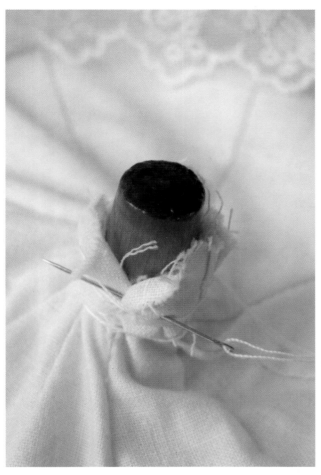 

Secure the cover around the top of the stick by sewing a row of gathering stitched around the top of the cover.

Add additional lace and glue the ferrule in place with PVA.

ADAPTING THE PARASOL

Parasols came in a variety of sizes and some were decorative rather than practical. To reduce the making time for the parasol in this chapter a child's frame could be used. A simpler version of the parasol could be made in a cotton stripe without lace trimming. A parasol could also be made in a contrasting fabric to match the day dress project in Chapter 8. To make a more elaborate parasol based on an example from Worthing Museum a smaller frame could be used, which could then be lined in mauve silk and covered in a layer of black lace. A mauve ribbon can be used to tie in a bow.

and glue in place. Catch the ends of the scalloped edges to the cover with a backstitch where the lace meets the seams – this will hold the lace in place when the parasol is held upside down.

Pull the gathering stitches at the top of the cover. Pull tight and wrap the thread around the ferrule before backstitching in place. Cover with a

layer of gathered lace and one final layer with the scalloped edge facing upwards towards the top of the ferrule. Place the ferrule on the top of the stick and glue in place. Tie the ribbon around the ferrule and create a bow, each loop of the bow measuring 10cm in length. Finally, tie the tasselled silk cord around the handle.

Chapter 12
Wearing Edwardian Fashion

For all women, no matter what their financial circumstances might be, dressing with care and attention was seen as a sign of good manners. Women knew that their clothing and shoes should be clean, their belts worn taut and their hair brushed and dressed. Rules of etiquette dictated what was to be worn for each occasion and how a woman should behave. This was an age where a respectable woman would perch in an upright position on a seat rather than relax in comfort. Lady Colin Campbell explained in Etiquette of Good Society, *'In the house a woman should sit still and not fidget however a man may change his position in an infinity of ways, lounge and loll and cross his legs.' Strongly worded advice was directed towards the schoolgirl in* Weldon's Practical Needlework*:*

> It is in very bad form to go to an afternoon party in morning costume. A girl may regard herself as too insignificant a being for it to matter much what she wears...but she should dress from the point of view of her hostess's importance, not from her own humility.

Time spent thinking about what to wear was a preoccupation of the Edwardian woman of financial means. It was not merely a matter of getting dressed – clothes had to sit on the body to achieve the desired silhouette. Ideas came from journals, department stores, society pages and letters between correspondents. The matter also taxed the minds of inventors and there are several examples of patented devices that were meant to assist the fashionable woman in this matter. Keeping a blouse neatly tucked into a

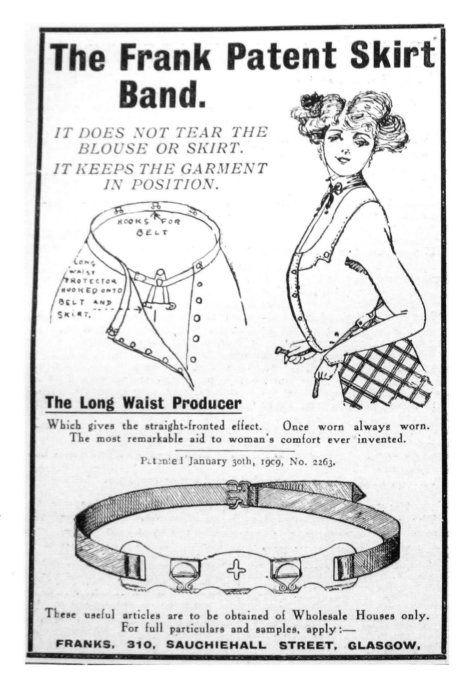

Advertisement for the Frank Patent Skirt Band, a patented device for holding a blouse neatly inside a skirt. (© EMap and the London College of Fashion Archive)

Left: A hand-painted sketch by Ida Pritchard of a woman wearing a blush pink gown with a lace overlay, and a large hat decorated with silk flowers. (Worthing Museum and Art Gallery)

skirt and pouched at the front led to the invention of patented skirt bands. In her memoir *Testament of Youth* Vera Brittain recalls a contraption worn during her Edwardian school days:

> We wore green flannel blouses in the winter and white flannel blouses in the summer, with long navy-blue skirts, linked to the blouses by elastic belts which continually slipped up or down, leaving exposed an unsightly hiatus of blouse-tape or safety-pinned shirt band.

The 'ZITA' Dip Front Adjuster features in *The Drapers' Record* in May 1902 and is said to make the waist look smaller while giving 'that charming dip-front or long waist effect now so essential.' In 1909 the problem still existed and The Frank Patent Skirt Band was said to be the most comfortable way of achieving a 'straight-fronted effect'.

ACCESSORIES

In *Victorian Costume* Anne Buck paid close attention to accessories as well as garments because she claimed that they were characteristic of the period. They were certainly an important element of the Edwardian woman's wardrobe; an ensemble would not have been complete without gloves – long for evenings and short for daywear. In 1905 Swan & Edgar's Ladies' Glove and Hosiery Department advertised day gloves in mocha suede or washing doeskin, while elbow-length evening gloves could be bought in kid or suede. A range of hose in black, tan or white was also available, held in place with elasticated garters trimmed with satin bows. In 1909 *The Lady's World* advised that fashionable boots and shoes 'must always have the "flat pitch" toe, and are mainly black, but occasionally carried out with patent vamps and coloured doeskin uppers to match the dress in question.' To keep the evening chills at bay real fur stoles and muffs were worn, feather boas and neck trims made from marabou and ostrich were also popular. Advertisements in women's journals and

Postcard of a fashionably dressed woman wearing a range of accessories and carrying a macramé bag, 1912. (Jayne Shrimpton)

trade catalogues show jewellery that was subtle and delicate: brooches worn at the front neck of a blouse, long strings of beads and pearls and contrasting, dangling earrings. There were also novelties in neckwear to pin to the front of a blouse or bodice. In April 1909 *The Drapers' Record* ran an advertisement for John Howell & Co., Ltd, who produced a range of narrow satin jabots with dangling bobbles at the ends or tassels; muslin, lace and glacé cravats and simple poplin ties.

Hats were an important element of an Edwardian woman's daily dress and consequently there were hats for all occasions and hats priced to suit all incomes. Edwardian rules of etiquette dictated that the head must be covered outdoors and so for outdoor wear hats were a necessity for women of all classes. The more elaborate hats required anchoring in place by the use of a pair of long steel hat pins. The pins were pushed through the hair and into 'rats' – the pad used to create extra volume in a woman's hair. In Vita

Sackville-West's novel, the following description is given of 'rats':

> They were unappetising objects, like last year's birds-nests, hot and stuffy to the head...they provided the foundation on which the coiffure was to be swathed and piled, and into which the innumerable hairpins were to be stuck. It was always a great source of preoccupation with the ladies that no bit of the pad should show through the natural hair.

The leisured lady of fashion emphasized her status with large hats as witnessed in *Isobel's Dressmaking at Home*, April 1901:

> Hats and toques are all large, one may almost say immense. Fancy straws of the willow order compose many of the newest crowns, and tucked glacé silk is also largely employed, and the toque partakes of the nature of a turban with a deep brim and large crown.

Large felt hat with oversized plumage sketched by Ida Pritchard. (Worthing Museum and Art Gallery)

Hat decorations continued to be lavish throughout the period. Inspiration was taken from nature and sometimes nature was directly added to hats, as in the case of birds. In April 1909 *The Drapers' Record* noted that the latest hats from Paris were trimmed with large, green, outstretched birds' wings or even a half side of a bird in the most exquisite colours. *The Drapers' Record* also noted, in 1909, the fashion in Paris for black hats, some huge, trimmed with bunches of roses that covered about a quarter of the hat. Flowers were popular hat decorations and at Shirley Leaf & Petal (the working artificial flower museum in the Sussex town of Hastings), catalogues and sample boards from 1910 show that small bunches of violets and large single roses were most in demand. Although millinery was a specialized occupation, women had the option to make their own hats. In the dressmaking journal *Weldon's Home Dressmaker* Mrs Pritchard gives instructions on making a velvet toque – a turban-style hat. She writes:

Toques can be constructed out of almost any material, from tulle and lace for summer and evening wear to velvet, cloth and fur, which, when artistically draped, forms a most suitable and cosy headgear for winter.

UNDERWEAR

The cleaning of a corset was a challenging process and so another layer that could be easily laundered was worn next to the skin, and this was the vest or chemise. The chemise was a long, sleeveless slip, which performed the function of a vest. Those observed in the museum collections appear to be made from cotton or linen. The better quality chemise might be embroidered around the neck with feather stich and have narrow, coloured ribbons threaded through broderie anglaise or lace. Clementina Black, in her survey of factory practices in *Married Women's*

Work, observed cheaper versions being made from flannelette or unbleached calico. Unbleached calico was described by one maker as 'the cheapest work' and she claimed it 'took more time to make up garments in it because the machine resisted the material. The chemise was worn tucked in to a pair of roomy drawers. Depending on the age and status of the wearer, Edwardian women had a choice of styles. Split drawers appeared in the early nineteenth century and although shortened in length, they were essentially just two separate legs reaching to the knee or sometimes beyond with fullness gathered onto a waistband that fastened at the back with ties. To ensure items of underclothing were always returned to their rightful owner after laundering, names and initials were sometimes elegantly embroidered on each piece; alternatively initials were crudely stitched in red thread.

Split drawers continued to be worn well into the Edwardian period. It is thought that younger women preferred closed drawers or knickers. Clementina Black observed women in London making drawers from flannelette and cotton. 'Knickers' was the term used by the women although Clementina Black stated that the garments were really drawers. In 1911, London department store D.H. Evans & Co were advertising 'French Peasant-made Longcloth Knickers, embroidered by hand' for sale at one shilling, eleven and a half pence. A further option was a pair of combinations, which were an all-in-one garment tapered to fit the upper half of the body. The advantage of combinations was the elimination of bulk around the waist.

With the underwear in place, the next layer would be a corset – this was something worn by all women, whatever their status. To go without a corset was very daring in an age defined by strict adherence to codes of etiquette. Lighter clothing often required an additional layer in the form of a camisole or corset cover. The camisole finished at the waist and was made from lightweight fabrics such as muslin or cotton batiste. They fastened down the front and were trimmed with lace and ribbons.

Worthing Museum has a selection of editions from the *Every-Woman's Encyclopaedia* and although not dated it can be noted by the style of garments featured that they date from approximately 1910. Lace blouses were transparent and it would not have been proper for the wearer to exhibit her corset worn underneath, so a camisole, or corset cover was worn as an additional layer over the corset and under the lace or net blouse. The *Every-Woman's Encyclopaedia* suggests a camisole with elbow-length sleeves as being particularly useful for wear under lace or transparent blouses. According to historian Alison Carter in her book *Underwear: The Fashion History*, the term 'brassiere' first appeared in American *Vogue* in 1907. As corsets began to drop downwards towards the waist the brassiere was introduced as a cover for the bare bosom rather than as a support to the bust. At this stage it did not have shaping and was a short loose tube with straps. Many were homemade and Worthing Museum has a pretty pink silk version with an embroidered motif and a large satin version made by an amateur dressmaker. C. Willett and Phillis Cunnington wrote in their book *The History of Underclothes*, 'The Edwardian petticoat was always flimsy; not more than two were worn, the top one, particularly when coloured, often being referred to as an underskirt'. In 1905 Swan & Edgar advertised the 'FanFan', a smart silk underskirt with bone casings, accordion pleating and a top flounce finished with frills. By 1908 with the introduction of the narrower skirt, full petticoats were reduced to a less bulky form. A sketch by the fashion illustrator Ida Pritchard that features in Chapter 5 is an example of the slim-line petticoat.

OUTERWEAR

Blouses

Blouses were made from wool, cotton, linen, lace, and both natural and artificial silks. Edwardian blouses signified feminine respectability and satisfied strict codes of etiquette in relation to dress. They were highly adaptable and were suitable for daywear and sportswear whilst still retaining the elegance of high fashion, with stylistic features often originally dictated by Parisian designers. Blouses were priced to suit all incomes and were widely available to purchase at department stores, or could be made by home dressmakers. The first blouses began to appear in and around 1890. At first they were fitted and boned but by 1900 lighter fabrics were used and the boning had disappeared. Blouse styles evolved through the Edwardian period and by 1906 the predominant style was a pouched front, with three-quarter-length full sleeves and a high collar.

Dress historian Norah Waugh states that blouse collars started to be boned from about 1900 when lighter weight net and lace was used in a single layer and not backed with stiff muslin, which had been the case since the 1890s. By 1905 boned collars were usual in blouses and gowns with lace collars –

in *Lucile Ltd: London, Paris, New York and Chicago, 1890s–1930s* Valerie Mendes and Amy de la Haye wrote, 'Almost all the 1905 day wear is worn over blouses with tall, stand-up or stock collars that compelled wearers to hold their head up high.' Collar supports were necessary in order to keep lightweight lace collars upright and taut. Celluloid, which has the appearance of yellow plastic, was the most commonly observed support in blouse collars during this research. An example observed in a blouse in Worthing Museum has celluloid supports measuring $3^1/_2$ inches long with holes at either end to enable attachment by hand stitching. They were uncovered and would have been extremely uncomfortable to the wearer. An alternative, and often longer, collar support was a flattened wire spring. Occasionally they were wrapped with thread but this offered little protection and would still leave the wire support pressed against the neck ready to pinch folds of skin with any movement of the head. Metal rods were also used and were sometimes successfully covered in fabric. In some cases the fabric was not thick enough to prevent the sharp tips of the rods from tearing through, ready to make contact with the neck causing physical pain, as expressed by Cynthia Asquith. In her memoir, *Remember and Be Glad*, she described the misery of

An example of metal collar supports used in a guipure lace blouse to keep the collar upright; one is missing and the other rusted support can be seen poking below the ribbon casing. (Worthing Museum and Art Gallery)

wearing boned collars in the early 1900s: 'I couldn't endure the high choking collars with boned supports that dug red dints in my neck, so I wore low square-necked blouses long before these became the fashion – a nonconformity for which I was severely criticised.'

Tailored costumes and skirts

The tailored costume, otherwise known as the tailored suit, was a useful and practical outfit for the Edwardian woman. Ladies' tailors, court dressmakers and furriers John Redfern and Sons, based in Cowes on the Isle of Wight, were suppliers of quality, upmarket outerwear and women of means could purchase sporting dress, morning gowns and daywear. At the cheaper end of the market the Manchester-based firm John Noble were advertising 'half-guinea costumes' in the second edition of penny weekly *Home Chat* published in 1895. The fitted bodice and matching skirt were 'the most remarkable value ever produced' at a price of 10s 6d. The skirt was also available to buy

Postcard (1910–1913) showing a woman in a two-piece costume wearing a large hat accessorized with a large flower. (Jayne Shrimpton)

separately at 5s 6d. Although only available to buy in one choice of fabric, Cheviot Serge, the customer had a choice of colours: black, navy, brown, myrtle, bronze-green, tan, grey or drab. The advertising feature makes reference to the story of the only female survivor of a shipwreck to attest to the durability of its fabric. The young woman, Miss Anna Boecker, survived the sinking of the *Elbe*, which went down very suddenly one morning in the North Sea. She was allegedly wearing a John Noble costume made from Cheviot Serge and despite being immersed in the water for five hours the costume had not shrunk. A comparison with newspaper reports at the time shows a different account: the captain of the ship that rescued the survivors spoke of seeing Miss Boecker lying on the floor of the lifeboat wearing only a long coat, having been pulled from the sea into the lifeboat after spending ten minutes in the freezing water.

Day dresses

The day dress reproduced in Chapter 8 is from the Farebrother collection at Royal Pavilion & Museums, Brighton & Hove. Similar striped cotton summer dresses feature in many Edwardian fashion editorials. A further example can be seen in the design from the Brighton fashion house Barrance and Ford and in an illustration by Ida Pritchard. A pretty selection of summer day dresses made from white cotton lawn with lace insertions can be seen at Royal Pavilion & Museums; they are similar to lightweight blouses with lace insertions and tucks. Another lightweight option was the tea-gown. Dress historian Norah Waugh in her book *The Cut of Women's Clothes* writes that in the period 1890–1908, 'Tea-gowns were loose and full, sometimes with "Watteau" back pleats or the Empire line, and with long, hanging sleeves.' Tea-gowns were worn in the afternoon when a woman wanted to feel comfortable at home and they were worn without a corset. The 'Empire' tea-gown was popular with *Isobel's Dressmaking at Home* in

1901 – just the thing to step into at home to escape the cold March winds. The dress was constructed over a princess lining with a voile overdress with fullness arranged in a Watteau pleat at the back. An elbow-length sleeve with frilled edge would enable the gown to be 'perfectly finished'. The fullness of the overdress can be imagined when noting six yards of voile or eleven yards of soft silk was needed to make the tea-gown. 'Heliotrope' was the suggested colour, with black and white embroideries. Worthing Museum has a pink pleated wool tea-gown with cream lace inserts; it is a loose-fitting, front-fastening garment with full sleeves, resembling a loose negligée. In November 1907 Mrs Pritchard's weekly column in *The Ladies' Field* advised readers of the importance of matching their tea-gown to their surroundings: the 'dark oak background and ample space' found in

Hand-painted fashion plate from Barrance and Ford showing a grey, black, white and brown day dress with a geometric trim applied around the hem of the skirt. (Peter Hinkins)

a large country house provided the perfect setting for a tea-gown of cerise, flame and orange. Mrs Pritchard appreciated the comfort provided by the tea-gown and accepted the lack of boning but preferred a tea-gown that defined the waistline. The tea-gown began to go out of fashion during the late Edwardian period; in 1909 *Lady's World* wrote:

> No one now wears the loose 'Empire' tea-gown, which every woman counted amongst her favourite, most comfortable garments not so long ago. The tea-gown in question was comfortable – there is no denying it – and it was often of beautiful material, daintily decorated. Its great drawback was its sloppy looseness, which utterly disguised the lines of the figure and which only very tall figures could carry well.

Evening gowns

Evening gowns were an ideal opportunity for displaying the Edwardian woman's love of embellishment. *The Ladies' Field* reported the craze for a more fitted and structured Empire-line gown amongst wealthy socialites in January 1906. Gowns cut in this style had a high waistline that was slanted to be lower at the front and higher at the back. A jet-beaded bolero finishing at the same height was apparently a fashionable accessory to complement the Empire-line gown in Monte Carlo.

Capes

Capes, cloaks and mantles were a useful way to wear an outer layer without disturbing and squashing the frills and flounces of the layer below. For Empire-line gowns a circular cape with an upturned 'half-moon' collar and low hood was suggested by the *Ladies' Supplement of the London Journal*, because the hood could be pulled up over the head when walking to the carriage. An opera cloak was a longer and equally voluminous alternative with long, loose sleeves. Opera cloaks finished below the knee and skimmed over the gown underneath, often flaring out at the hem. In November 1906 *The Ladies' Field* suggested pastel tones were desirable for an evening coat, made from wool satin with a silk lining and an interlining of domette for extra warmth.

Sporting clothes

In March 1889 *The Ladies' Field* wrote of the revival of women's sports in the late nineteenth century. They attributed this to better diets and outdoor living. *The Ladies' Field* contained a sports section – 'sports and pastimes' – a serious item of journalism that reported the statistics and achievements of women who excelled in their sport. Sporting dress was not mentioned in this section; readers had to consult the fashion pages for ideas. As sporting activities developed women wore and adapted their own clothing for playing outdoor sport but by the Edwardian period specific sports clothing was available to buy from department stores or could be made by the home dressmaker. Sports clothing design was based around the fashions of the day, although there were some concessions to comfort and ease of movement in the design of corsets.

Lawn tennis was popular with those who could afford the fees at membership-only tennis clubs. White was a popular colour for tennis dress because it disguised perspiration marks better than coloured fabrics. As well as the tennis dress, accessories were adapted and designed specifically for the game and the tennis racquet motif appeared on aprons with pockets used for carrying balls and on belts. The skirt and shirt combination was just the thing for the female golfer, especially when accessorized with a masculine-inspired tie and a simple beret.

WEARING THE CLOTHES AND ACCESSORIES IN THE BOOK

The garments and accessories in the book form a capsule collection – although this was not a term in use in the Edwardian period – with pieces that can be combined to create new outfits and adapted for a range of situations and characters. The outfits might be suitable for an Edwardian governess, a campaigning suffragette, a passenger on an ocean liner or a woman overseeing a busy household in large country house. The underwear – the drawers, chemise and petticoat – can be worn with all clothes with the exception of the evening gown. Patterns are cut for a modern shape but to achieve an authentic look a boned corset should be worn with all outfits, with the exception of the evening dress when a lighter corset can be worn. The white lace blouse can be worn with the plain skirt from the walking dress with the addition of a belt, or with the striped skirt from the day dress. The detachable black tie from the day dress can be worn at the front of the blouse collar. The velvet toque, a feather boa and a knitted or macramé Dorothy bag could be added to this ensemble to complete the look. The cape can be worn over the day dress or a combination of the blouse and a skirt. The day dress can also be accessorized with the lace parasol and the velvet toque; a pair of white, short, cotton lace gloves could also be worn. The beaded evening bag complements the evening gown. The evening gown can also be accessorized with long black gloves, black silk hose and a delicate headdress made from feathers and beads.

Suppliers

Vena Cava (suppliers of costume-making equipment and parasol frames)
PO Box 3597, Poole, Dorset BH14 9ZL
Website: www.venacavadesign.co.uk
Email: info@venacavadesign.co.uk

Ditto Fabrics
21 Kensington Gardens, Brighton
BN1 4AL
Website: https://dittofabrics.co.uk
Phone: 01273 603771

Fabric Land (fabrics)
76 Western Road, Brighton, East Sussex
BN1 2HA
Website: www.fabricland.co.uk
Phone: 01425 461444
Email: maxine.fabricland@gmail.com

Depotex (fabrics)
16 Fisher Street, Lewes BN7 2DG
Phone: 01273 487956

Merchant and Mills (fabrics and sewing equipment)
14A Tower Street, Rye, East Sussex
TN31 7AT
Website: http://merchantandmills.com
Phone: 01797 227789

Simply Sequins (online sequin shop)
82 Durrants Road, Rowlands Castle,
Hampshire PO9 6BG
Website: www.simplysequins.co.uk
Phone: 023 9247 6125
Email: sales@simplysequins.co.uk

Wayward (new and vintage fabrics and trimmings)
68 Norman Road, St Leonards on Sea,
East Sussex TN38 0EJ
Website: http://wayward.co
Phone: 07815 013337
Email: info@wayward.co

Jaycotts (sewing equipment)
Unit D2, Chester Trade Park, Bumpers
Lane, Chester, Cheshire CH1 4LT
Website: www.jaycotts.co.uk
Phone: 01244 394099
Email: alex@jaycotts.co.uk

William Gee (pattern cutting paper and sewing equipment)
520–522 Kingsland Road, London
E8 4AH
Website: www.williamgee.co.uk
Phone: 0207 254 2451
Email: info@williamgee.co.uk

The Bead Shop Brighton
21 Sydney Street, Brighton BN1 4EN
Website: http://beadsunlimited.co.uk
Phone: 01273 675077
Email: shop@beadsunlimited.co.uk

Anne Tomlin (flower artist, makes flowers to order and runs classes in flower making; also gives individual tuition)
Email: aetomlin@gmail.com

Lomax and Skinner (milliners who make bespoke hats, run classes and give individual tuition at their workshop)
66 The High Street, Lewes, East Sussex
BN7 1XG
Website: www.lomaxandskinner.co.uk
Phone: 07949 123693
Email: studio@lomaxandskinner.co.uk

Morplan (sewing equipment)
Unit 1, Temple Bank, Harlow, Essex
CM20 2DY
Website:
www.morplan.com/shop/en/morplan
Phone: 0800 451122
Email: web.support@morplan.com

Bibliography

BOOKS

Arnold, Janet (1982). *Patterns of Fashion 2: Englishwomen's Dresses and Their Construction c.1860–1940*. Macmillan.

Asquith, Cynthia (1952). *Remember and Be Glad*. Charles Scribner's Sons.

Black, Clementina (1915). *Married Women's Work*. London: G. Bell and Sons.

Brittain, Vera (1978). *Testament of Youth*. Virago.

Buck, Anne (1984). *Victorian Costume*. Ruth Bean Publishers.

Campbell, Lady Colin (1912). *Etiquette of Good Society*. Cassell.

Carter, Alison (1992). *Underwear: The Fashion History*. London: B.T. Batsford Ltd.

Earnshaw, Pat (1982). *A Dictionary of Lace*. Shire Publications.

Hopkins, J.C. (1990). *Edwardian Ladies' Tailoring: The Twentieth Century System of Ladies' Garment Cutting* (1910). R.L. Shep.

Hunnisett, Jean (1988). *Period Costumes for Stage and Screen: Patterns for Women's Dress 1800–1909*. Unwin Paperbacks.

Mendes, Valerie D. and de la Haye, Amy (2009). *Lucile Ltd: London, Paris, New York and Chicago, 1890s–1930s*. V&A Publishing.

Meyer, Mrs Carl and Black, Clementina (1909). *Makers of our Clothes*. Duckworth & Co.

Sackville-West, Vita (1983). *The Edwardians*. Virago Modern Classics.

Smith, Amy K. (1910). *Cutting Out for Student Teachers*. Sir Isaac Pitman & Sons Ltd.

Taylor, Lou (2002). *The Study of Dress History*. Manchester University Press.

Walker, Agnes (1907). *How to Make up Garments*. Blackie & Sons Ltd.

Waugh, Norah (1994). *The Cut of Women's Clothes: 1600–1930*. Faber and Faber.

Willett C. and Cunnington, Phillis (1992). *The History of Underclothes*. Dover Publications Inc.

Woman's Institute of Domestic Arts & Sciences, Scranton, PA:
Embroidery and Decorative Stitches (1916)
The Dressmaker and Tailor's Shop (1917)
Underwear and Lingerie (1921)
Essential Stitches and Seams (1922)
Tailored Seams and Plackets (1923)

PERIODICALS

The Ladies' Field
Home Chat
The Drapers' Record
The Lady's World
Isobel's Dressmaking at Home
Weldon's Home Dressmaker
Weldon's Illustrated Dressmaker
Weldon's Practical Needlework
The Queen
Woman's World

MUSEUMS VISITED FOR RESEARCH

Royal Pavilion & Museums, Brighton & Hove
Worthing Museum and Art Gallery
Museum of London
The Clothworkers' Centre for the Study and Conservation of Textiles

Acknowledgements

This book would not have been possible without the kindness and support of Martin Pel, Curator of Fashion and Textiles at Royal Pavilion & Museums, Brighton & Hove, and Gerry Connolly, Curator of Historic Collections at Worthing Museum and Art Gallery. Both curators gave generous access to the wonderful collections at their respective museums and shared their expertise. I am also grateful to Professor Lou Taylor who first inspired my interest in Edwardian fashion by guiding me towards the production and consumption of Edwardian blouses, which became the subject of my MA dissertation. I am grateful to the following museums and archives for allowing research at their collections: Museum of London, University of Brighton Design Archives, London College of Fashion Archive and The Clothworkers' Centre for the Study and Conservation of Textiles.

I am indebted to costume designer Frances Tempest and theatrical tailor and cutter Tony Rutherford for sharing professional tips, and Stephanie Richards for reading my introduction and offering comments. Many thanks to Jayne Shrimpton and to Katharine Williams for supplying Edwardian photographs and giving permission to publish, and to Peter Hinkins for giving permission to reproduce fashion plates from the Barrance and Ford, Brighton Ltd, catalogue. I am also grateful to EMap for allowing the publication of images from *The Drapers' Record* Archive, and to Worthing Museum and Art Gallery for permission to publish images from the collection of fashion illustrator Ida Pritchard and from their collection of dressmaking manuals and journals. Further thanks are due to Marion May who kindly showed me her Edwardian dress collection and gave permission for the reproduction of images.

I am very grateful to Karen Cunningham for skilfully cutting the finished patterns and to skilled costume maker Kate Stallion for helping with costume making. Many thanks to costumier Rachel Woolcott, who made such a good job of beading the evening bag and helped to make the split drawers. Jo Lance, design history graduate and milliner, did a great job of making the velvet toque, and the beautiful flower was researched and made by flower artist Anne Tomlin. I would also like to thank Simon Barclay at Depotex fabric shop in Lewes for advising on fabrics.

I am grateful to Benjamin Rowland for taking photographs for chapter openers and for editing my photographs. Thank you also to photographer Andrew Perris who photographed the finished underwear and walking dress. Many thanks to illustrator Joe McCrae who sketched the original museum garments and to Zachary Rowland who sketched the measurements guide.

Finally, I would like to thank Chris Rowland who adapted his CAD drawing skills to reduce the patterns, and provided endless cups of tea and support.

Index

accessories
    making 104–117
    wearing 120–122
Asquith, Cynthia, Edwardian memoirs 9, 57–58, 122–123
alterations and repairs 21

beading
    beading techniques 22, 91–95, 105–108
    evening bag 105–107
    evening gown 92–95
beeswax 18
bobbles 21
bodkin 18
boning 86
brush braid 30
buttons and buttonholes, two-part walking dress bodice 64

chemise 36–39
collars
    blouse, lace collar 54–55
    cape 99–103
    collar supports 77, 81, 122–123
    day dress, lace collar 77–78, 81
    two-part walking dress 66–67
cutting and layout
    blouse 50–51
    cape 98–99
    chemise 37
    day dress 69–73
    evening bag 106
    evening gown 85–89
    flower motif, evening gown 93
    neck tie, day dress 78
    parasol 115
    petticoat 43–44
    split drawers 34–35
    two-part walking dress bodice 63
    two-part walking dress, skirt 58–59
    velvet toque 109–110

darts
    cape, open darts 99
    petticoat, closed darts 44
department stores offering made-to-measure, history 10–12
drafting paper 17
dress stand 19

Edwardian dressmaking history 12–13, 49
Edwardian silhouette 9
Empire tea-gown, history 123–124
epaulets and strappings, day dress 76–77
evening bag, making 105–108

fabrics
    Edwardian colours and prints 25–26
    glossary of fabrics 26–29
    sourcing fabrics 25
faggoting 21
Farebrother, Katherine, Edwardian clothing 10

fittings 21
flounce
    flounce for cape 100
    flounce for petticoat 43, 46
foundation bodice, evening gown 86–87
Fray Check 17
frill, petticoat 45, 47

gathering, chemise 38
Gibson Girl 10
glossary of fabrics 26–29
grain lines 21

hats, history 120–121
hat making project, see toque
hem facings 21
    day dress, bias cut hem facing 78
    two-part walking dress, shaped hem facing 63
hooks and bars, day dress 81

insertion lace 51
interfacing and boning 29

measurements guide 25,31
millinery wire hat frame, making 110–111
museum research 7

neck tie 78
needles for hand sewing 17
Noble, John, half-guinea costumes 123

parasol, making 113–117
parasols, Worthing Museum 113–114
patterns
    adding seam allowance 16
    Edwardian patterns, history 19–20
    enlarging 16,23
    grain lines 21
    making a toile to test fit 16
    sizes 25
    taking patterns from existing garments 20
peplum, day dress 77
pin-tucks 22
    blouse 52–53
    petticoat 46
plackets 61, 79
pockets
    cape patch pocket 101
    skirt patch pocket, two-part walking dress 62–63
    skirt placket hole pocket, two-part walking dress 59–60
    skirt watch pocket, two-part walking dress 62
pressing tools and techniques 16
Pritchard, Mrs Eric, Edwardian fashion journalist 9, 123
Pritchard, Ida, Edwardian fashion illustrator 6, 11 ,49, 83

quilted cape lining 101

rolling and whipping 21
rouleau loop 102
ruffles, cape 100–101
Rutherford, Tony, tips from a theatrical cutter and tailor 23

scarf, evening gown 92
scissors 16–17
seam allowance, adding to patterns 15, 17
seams
    Edwardian seams 21
    faggoting 54
    flat felled 35, 39
    French 44, 116
    open 99
sleeves
    blouse sleeve with inserts 54
    draped, evening gown 90,95
    setting in 65–66, 76
    two-piece, two-part walking dress 64–65
sewing machines 19
side panels, evening gown 92
silhouette 9, 15
skirt band, for holding a blouse inside a skirt 119–120
Smith, Amy K., *Cutting Out for Student Teachers* (1910) 36
split drawers 33–36
sporting clothes, history 124

tacking techniques 20–21
tape measure 17
Tempest, Frances, tips from a costume designer 23
thimble 18
toque 109–113
tracing wheel 18
trimmings 30
tucks 22
    blouse 52–53
    chemise 37–38
    day dress 73–74
    two-part walking dress 66–67

underskirt, evening gown 90–91
underwear
    how underwear was worn 33, 121–122
    making drawers 33–36
    making the chemise 36–39

waistbands
    day dress 80
    Petersham 29
    split drawers 35–36
    two-part walking dress 61
waist stay 11, 84
Walker, Agnes, *How to Make Up Garments* (1907) 36